A
Social
Action
Primer

BOOKS BY DIETER T. HESSEL
Published by The Westminster Press

Reconciliation and Conflict: Church
    Controversy Over Social Involvement

A Social Action Primer

A
Social
Action
Primer

by
DIETER T. HESSEL

THE WESTMINSTER PRESS
Philadelphia

BOOK DESIGN BY
DOROTHY ALDEN SMITH

Published by The Westminster Press ®
Philadelphia, Pennsylvania

PRINTED IN THE UNITED STATES OF AMERICA

Library of Congress Cataloging in Publication Data

Hessel, Dieter T
    A social action primer.

    Includes bibliographical references.
    1. Social action. 2. Church and social problems.
I. Title.
HN17.5.H48   301.24   72-77325
ISBN 0-664-24957-4

To Allison and Tracy
daughters who deserve, and will see
the need for, social change
as soon as possible

CONTENTS

CONTENTS

FOREWORD

I began a set of notes for this book while teaching an ethics course entitled "Strategies and Styles of Social Action," at the Graduate Theological Union, Berkeley, California. Throughout the course I was impressed with three circumstances: (1) the perplexity of many would-be social actors, (2) the lack of available literature on the subject, and (3) the tendency of some approaches to social ethics to ignore citizen action.

The participants in "Strategies and Styles of Social Action," mostly beginning theological students, came out of several Protestant and Catholic traditions and reflected diverse views of social reality. But they shared considerable uncertainty about being able to make a social difference even while they expressed a common desire to become competent change agents in society. I invited them to explore ways of social action pertinent to the issues that concerned them.

We subdivided into teams (or task groups) each of which focused on a specific issue with the objective of planning or evaluating an action program. This procedure was intended to open up strategic moral thought in a social dimension chosen by each student. Early in the

process I presented a frame of reference—a theory of social action practice—and met separately with most of
the teams outside scheduled class time. In later sessions
some of the teams reported to the class what they had
learned, emphasizing either the action plan they helped to
devise or their evaluation of an existing action program
with which they made contact. Issue areas explored included: peace education, draft counseling, suburban racism, campaign advertising on television, community control of police, the status of women in the church, and
patterns of community organization. The reports tended
to be more *narrative* of the problem or program than
analytical about the action strategy. The students found
it difficult to identify and scrutinize the strategic choices
evident in particular action plans. As the quarter ended,
we had only begun to develop strategic consciousness.

Thus the course itself illustrated a common educational
problem. School does not prepare us to think rigorously
about modes of action for social change. High school and
college orient us to *discussion* of written material about
social issues. Unfortunately, the available literature, except for bits and pieces, does little to develop *action* insight. The mass of printed and audio-visual material continues to expose a myriad of policy issues and institutional
failures, or generally describes movements for change.
Such material appears unceasingly, because movements
and issues constantly take new forms. In order that we
may avoid a paralysis of issue analysis, we need personal
exposure to social action opportunities and explicit treatment of social action philosophy.

Unable to find an introduction to the subject in a current and available format, I wrote my own. This job
could undoubtedly be done better by a prominent practi-
tioner of the art. But most of the noted social action lead-

ers have written little or, like Martin Luther King, Jr., have been silenced. (King provided the classic account of the Montgomery bus boycott in *Stride Toward Freedom: The Montgomery Story;* Harper & Row, Publishers, Inc., 1958.) So it was necessary to implement a familiar action guideline—you often have to fill a need rather than wait for someone more "expert."

My social action experience, although limited, is informed by a background of study in the field of ethics and several years of professional participation in one kind of voluntary organizational setup—a major American Protestant denomination. Elsewhere I have written about the pattern of conflict the church experiences as it attempts to play a responsible social action role. (*Reconciliation and Conflict: Church Controversy Over Social Involvement;* The Westminster Press, 1969.) In this primer a review of the church's social action role is reserved for the last chapter.

Responsiveness to public issues is not a unique obligation or opportunity for a single kind of organization; rather, it is a common human task in every sector of society. Therefore, this book employs a vocabulary that is usable in any class, community group, corporate setting, or citizen organization.

To focus on the social action process is a straightforward way to do social ethics. It overcomes a general preoccupation on the part of the ethics "establishment" with analyzing the language of moral discourse or the dilemmas of top policy decision makers. A focus on social action, by contrast, highlights conditions of citizen impotence and requirements for group effectiveness in shaping public policy. The crucial question is: How shall ordinary folks influence social policy?

In other words, we can shift attention away from explaining the behavior of the rulers to exploring the social interests and action tasks of the ruled. This makes ethics more strategic in meeting the crisis of participation that confronts every would-be change agent. Rather than imagining ourselves at the right hand of major policy makers, we explore the values and virtues of change agentry where *we* meet the issues. (For example, instead of wondering, "What would I do as governor?" we ask, "How can we have some influence on a particular policy choice?")

I am indebted to San Francisco Theological Seminary for inviting me to try out this approach at the Graduate Theological Union, and I am also grateful to the United Presbyterian Board of Christian Education for granting the study leave that made it possible for me to take advantage of that opportunity.

Words in a thoughtful vein about the social action process are especially important now since: (*a*) prominent public figures tend to condemn "activism" and to propose trite, or overly narrow, definitions of "legitimate" action, (*b*) few leaders of groups have actually been through the ABC's of the subject, and (*c*) newcomers and veterans to the field often show disdain for one another's strategies and tactics.

Feel free to add your own insights and corrections to this presentation. This primer, like every discussion of social action, is incomplete; and on this subject everyone who acts gains some expertise and has something to contribute. The crucial thing is to convey the art to others, so more people in groups will exercise social action imagination and discipline.

D. T. H.

A
Social
Action
Primer

1

BEYOND APATHY AND REVOLT

This is a handbook for change agents. It is addressed primarily to those who desire a new order of personal and political values, and who want to help make these values operational. This book is intended to encourage disciplined, sustained social action.

Such action can occur wherever we are. Whatever our occupations, our common business is to reshape social institutions and public policies to serve humane ends. Many of us will lead, or already lead, voluntary organizations. In our occupations and associations we are capable of influencing the design and direction of political, economic, and social structures. Given ample opportunities for social action, the question is whether we will participate in public affairs or leave the job entirely in the hands of a few others.

A healthy society depends on people learning the art of associating together for purposes of social transformation. This is not a new political imperative, just a more urgent one. A century and a half ago, in his study of American society, Alexis de Tocqueville warned: "If men are to remain civilized or to become so, the art of associating together must grow and improve in the same ratio in which the equality of conditions is increased. . . . If each citizen did not learn, in proportion as he individually becomes more feeble, and consequently more incapable of preserving his freedom single-handed, to combine with his fellow citizens for the purpose of defending it, it is clear that tyranny would unavoidably increase with equality."

Since demands for equality gain momentum even while the means of social control become more sophisticated, will it be the best or the worst of times? Is democratic pluralism achievable or is repressive order unavoidable? Is the social system breaking through or breaking down? Amitai Etzioni points to the ambiguous forces at work in our situation: "Man is reaching a new phase in which his ability to obtain freedom, as well as his ability to subjugate others, is greatly extended. Both of these build on his increasing capacity to transform social bonds rather than accommodate to, or merely protest, the social patterns he encounters." [1]

Toward an Active Society?

The times require much wider participation by citizens in the process of community formation and governance. Yet, just as there are more people who want to take charge of their future, there is also an increase in the number who quietly acquiesce to the holders of power. Far from threatening to rebel, they succumb to *in*action. Among them one senses a *post-activist* mood—a weariness with the struggle for justice, a lack of hope for positive institutional change.

The early '70s have brought a noticeable reduction in public protest and a slowdown of social reform. Does this mean the "death" of social action? Don't bet on it!

One lesson we should have learned from the '60s is that successive half decades are not alike. Cycles are shorter, including periods of quietism. Less visible action in the early '70s may be due to readjustment, rather than exhaustion. Amid richer pluralism of movements and life-styles, it is necessary to cast about for meaningful channels of action. The outcome could be less romantic, more realistic efforts by organized groups to change the priorities of institutions and governments.

Of course, there is strong sentiment to return to the old order, to hold to ways of thinking and governing rooted in earlier decades. Sentiment for the old order makes itself felt in reaction to each new push toward political and economic justice. Yet, no holding actions can long prevent the newer dynamics from breaking through.

A most impressive structural fact is that about sixty million young people come of age between 1968 and 1980.[2] The '70s is the decade when the counter-culture enters the institutional and political mainstream. It is also the decade of extensive community self-organization among America's blacks, Chicanos, Asians, and Indians. These developments will shake the old order again. In addition, more people who are neither young nor poor are beginning to express their loss of confidence in established social arrangements and conventional remedies for social ills. They perceive that current institutional practices and governmental policies create large pockets of poverty, produce middle-class malaise, and cannot seem to reverse a general deterioration of public services and community life. They also see the lack of decent housing, transportation, and environment, and the failure to produce a healthy educational system. They too are disturbed that our government has spent hundreds of billions of dollars for killing in Indochina, whereas it would not provide minimally for jobs and income to raise millions of families above the poverty level. They also recognize that everywhere our social system wastes people and resources.

In this milieu, social action is *more,* not less, likely. But it must be initiated. Group initiatives for social change— often *ad hoc,* featuring a mix of laymen and "experts"— are part of our civil tradition. Voluntary modes of action are characteristic of mature individuals and a healthy body politic.

To borrow a term from psychologist A. H. Maslow, a healthy society is shaped by people who are "self-actualizing" in both their private and political relationships. Maslow has observed that human development moves from "lower" to "higher" order needs. As man meets his lower needs (subsistence, safety, belonging, and recognition), his energies are freed for actualizing his higher needs (to explore freedom, to express creativity, and to build community). Self-actualizing people commit their talents to some cause outside the self, such as the quest for beauty, truth, and justice. They reach human maturity in the process of working for these larger goals.[3]

Similarly, authentic democracy features the participation of persons and groups in the making of those social policies that affect their destiny. Not that the voice of the people always reflects the wisest preferences (since the people can be swayed in the short run by misinformation and propaganda). But a leadership subject to the will of the people is more likely to meet their needs than does either a technocratic or a revolutionary elite that presumes to know what is best for them. Even the cynic Machiavelli observed that only in functioning republics is the common good looked to properly.

However, the object of this book is not to extol democracy in the abstract. Our purpose is to make democracy work for us and for our brothers. Whatever the official rhetoric, most of us know that the social policy-making system has not worked well enough to secure quality of life or to give every citizen real access to the necessities of life. Injustice and alienation abound. There are grievances to redress, priorities to establish, and institutions to reform.

In other words, the democratic process needs to be and can be revitalized. It is battered and even messy; but it is a durable method of institutional and public government that is capable of finding proximate solutions to seemingly insoluble problems, provided that enough people know what is happening (free speech and free press are crucial) and engage the issues without fear of governmental harassment. (Liberty always gives way to authority unless liberty is exercised and defended.) Where these conditions exist there is opportunity for authentic social involvement—what Ralph Nader has dubbed "initiatory democracy." [4]

The people should take the initiative to make the system work. But it is also incumbent upon public officials and corporate managers to revise the system so that morally desirable results are evident, and to observe restraint of power and due process of law, so that people can go on working for the civil goals that matter. (This suggests that the social action process includes conserving as well as transforming tasks. It can mean resisting or initiating public policies, and often both thrusts together.)

Staying with It

In the field of social action there is rather widespread disillusionment and disorientation. A recent college graduate exemplifies this condition in the complaint, "I've tried social action and it doesn't work!" Were it not so common, this judgment would be laughable, based as it is on the results of a few brief skirmishes. The student had joined a couple of disappointing demonstrations. Since he apparently had not accomplished anything, he proposed to turn from the grand issues to the small, the individual, the personal.

Such quickly disillusioned people would probably benefit from an analytical discussion of the limits of mass demonstrations and the merits of other action tactics. In recognition of such a need, this book contains a chapter entitled "Analyzing Tactics." Thus one can begin to distinguish between positive acts of confrontation designed to change the system in the direction of justice, and an impotent stance of rejection that merely protests a repressive or toxic environment. Yet, analyzing tactics does not necessarily touch the source of disillusion. The notion that social action is unworkable may arise from personal needs rather than from lack of know-how. The quest for meaning—a religious problem—enters directly into the picture.

On the one hand, we share an intensified quest for what, besides bread, makes life abundant. Human community, we now understand, is harder to gain than material goods. Particularly important but elusive in group life are the qualities of celebration, thoughtfulness, and grace. Why shouldn't these qualities be cultivated even while we work for justice? Must participants in the social action process be frazzled and manipulative, their language self-justifying, their tactics savage? This is *not* a proposal to subordinate social action strategy to the human development movement. (After all, trust-building is no substitute for redistributing power.) But we are reminded that no amount of political technique can overcome spiritual emptiness at the heart of a change strategy or among the people who act.

On the other hand, some have tried to achieve personal salvation through action. Theirs has been a quest for revelation, not reform. This was vividly exemplified at the turn of the decade when there was so much revolutionary posturing. Being together in protest seemed to be far more personally satisfying than working within the system. Given the international situation and accumulating crises at home, the search for salvation through dramatic action was not surprising. It was tempting to hope that in action one could find personal integrity, a purity of deed over against rotting institutions.

But the "Pure Protestors," as Michael Novak dubbed them, could only flit from one flare-up to the next. Such revolutionary fervor quickly waned. Said one young revolutionary: "I guess last year we really believed the apocalypse was the day after tomorrow. When it didn't come, we sort of retreated to the day after yesterday. Now we know that things are bleak, but we know that we have thirty or forty years of life ahead of us, and we have to deal with that."

An adequate social action process will respond to the need for both personal well-being and systemic change. It will concentrate on engendering styles of change agentry that are personally rewarding and have staying power in the struggle to restructure social institutions and public policies. Above all, social action leaders will help people focus on effective ways to achieve decision-making power and a fair distribution of resources (i.e., to achieve political and economic justice).

There will be no easy victories. In fact, there are few decisive battles at all, only opportunities for people who are organized to influence the direction of institutions and policies.

Effective social involvement requires both perception and staying power, both skill and spirit, both technique and vision. The actionist considers what the future ought to be and not just what is wrong with the present or how to get marginal reform. While he analyzes, Who has the "clout"? he also ponders, What do we want to become? and, How can we move in that direction? He projects a human future and works to form it. "Imagination sees that things should stop being as they are; man goes ahead of the existing conditions of the present. He transcends the facts and therefore gains the distance needed to drag the facts along the direction chosen by his will, through his activity." [5]

Possible Consequences of Social Inaction

Our society is now in a crucial transition brought on by the pace of technological change. Biophysicist John Platt presents these figures to dramatize the pace of change:

In the last century, we have increased our speeds of communication by a factor of 10^7; our speeds of travel by 10^2; our speeds of data handling by 10^6; our energy resources by 10^3; our power of weapons by 10^6; our ability to control diseases by something like 10^2; and our rate of population growth by 10^3 times what it was a few thousand years ago. Could anyone suppose that human relations around the world would not be affected to their very roots by such changes? [6]

Platt perceives the thrust of the technological engine to be approaching a critical stage, like the shuddering lift-off of a space-bound rocket. During the lift-off, many crisis points are reached in rapid succession. Will we get through the transition intact, or will spaceship earth come apart during the next few decades? Platt presents a crisis intensity chart headed by the nuclear arms race, the demand for participatory democracy, the struggle to distribute food, to reverse ecological ruin, and to administer law humanely. There is no escaping problems of this scale. We are collectively in a game that we will all *lose* in nuclear holocaust, race war, or economic imperialism; or *win* together in survival and prosperity. To cope with this situation we need much more open education and social invention.

The contours of some urgent societal needs are sharpened when current trends are projected ahead ten or twenty years, creating what amounts to a "bad trip" into the future. Such a bad trip assumes a continuation of present policies without major alteration. Thus, William L. Taylor, former Staff Director of the U.S. Civil Rights Commission, sees dismal prospects for urban centers—namely, heightened deprivation, racial separation, and intergroup conflict. He notes that by 1985 there will probably be at least 178 million persons in U.S. metropolitan areas. Suburbs will contain 112.5 million residents, of whom 94 percent will be white. The central cities will contain 65.5 million residents of whom one third (on the average) will be nonwhite. The largest cities will be predominantly nonwhite "poor houses," deserted by many businesses, industries, and upper-income whites. The central cities will be unable to pay for adequate public services, including education, and their twenty million nonwhite residents will face shrinking opportunity and higher unemployment. There will be some further transfer of power to nonwhites in positions of political responsibility, but whites in the suburbs can still dilute black power in central cities by sheer weight of numbers and various redistricting techniques. The general process of urban deformation "threatens to grind up those black political leaders who are committed to reform through the democratic process [and to displace them with] a new brand of leadership—one which repudiates democratic processes that have failed and opts instead for violence." [7]

If this picture of two societies, separate and unequal but linked in disorders, is not threatening enough, other writers such as Christopher Lasch wonder if our institutional myopia and high technology have not already induced political *rigor mortis.*

The cities, where most of the people live, have become almost uninhabitable, and their problems increasingly appear insoluble within the conventional framework. Ghettos of misery and deprivation, the cities smolder until one of them burst into fire. . . . Poverty has not been eliminated, it has merely been concealed. Because they are both "invisible" and voiceless, the millions of poor have no way of making their presence felt except by violence; but precisely because they are leaderless and unorganized, violence, once it erupts, cannot be directed by radicals toward political objectives. Meanwhile the public safety seems to many Americans to require increasingly repressive measures on the part of a State whose powers have already dangerously expanded, and which finds itself inextricably involved in similar police actions abroad.[8]

Lasch doubts that more of the same police force, welfare measures, or wasteful technology will help to liberate the cities or to liquidate an overseas empire. To cope with turmoil, inequality, and scarcity, social priorities and institutional practices will have to be reshaped in a major way.

Major restructuring of the society is the broad goal of those who envision the reconciliation of mankind, and who therefore work for shared decision-making power and a fair distribution of resources. However, such change agents will be resisted at every hand by those who do not see the shared destiny and who fear the loss of their goods and privileges. Refusing to share their gains, the fearful actually risk much greater loss.

Etzioni warns that either we will have an *active society* of responsive people and organizations, and broadly shared control of the means of change; or we will have an *inauthentic society* dominated by alienating technological structures, 1984-style leadership, and much false awareness. This, of course, is a matter of emphasis and direction. No society or sector of society is either completely activated or completely inauthentic. The moral qualities of the two contrasting societies and their leaders can be grasped in the following oversimplified typology:

Inauthentic Society	*Activated Society*
Deprives	Equalizes
Alienates	Responds
Excludes	Includes
Fragments	Coalesces
Manipulates	Educates
Subjugates	Liberates
Destroys	Builds

The behavior of individuals and groups in the society is crucial to the outcome.

In the inauthentic society, the *majority* of the members are caught in the typical cleavage between their private selves and public roles and manage by treating their neuroses with drugs, alcohol, professional counseling, and the like, thus reinforcing the inauthenticity of the society which caused their malaise. There is a *minority* of retreatists who ignore their public roles and build lives around their private selves. While these people are more authentic and, potentially, carriers of societal change, they have little societal effect. *Finally* there are those who evolve new public selves which they collectivize and make the basis of their societal action. In these lies the hope for an initiation of the transformation of the inauthentic society. They are the active ones.[9]

2

WHAT IS SOCIAL ACTION?

In the previous chapter we emphasized that social action is important to the democratic process and a factor in the movement of history. Chapter 1 also offered a preliminary description of the task. Social action is the art of working together for the purpose of transforming society. Social action is involvement in efforts to reshape social institutions and public policies. It should be judged primarily by its effectiveness in achieving political and economic justice, though one should not ignore what it does to the people involved. It requires both skill and spirit. But precisely what is it? We are ready for a more careful definition.

Social action is a process of deliberate group effort to alter community or societal structures for the common good.

Unpacking the Definition

Notice *first* of all that we are talking about a *process,* a continuous change effort. Social action on any issue typically means trying to alter a sector of "the system" by reducing the facade of institutional injustice and by constructing better policies. It can be hard work, requiring sustained effort, as former Secretary of the Interior Walter J. Hickel observed in a letter (dated October 23, 1970) to a young leader of an environmental-action group.

Many of the youth of today have learned that change is not an instant thing. They know you cannot "add water and stir" and solve the ingrained prejudice and indifference of people, the cruelty of the inner cities, and the desecration of our natural environment. Maturity in the sense of effective social change has very little to do with age.

Perseverance is part of the process. So is selectivity. One has to choose among the many issues that should be engaged and all the groups that could be joined. (See Chapter 5 for some guidelines in making these choices.) Issues and movements confront us in constantly changing form, like the shifting patterns in a kaleidoscope. This is the main content of the daily news. But social action has more substance than any momentary combination of public issues or of social movements. The process of altering social structures, with all its variations, is rather stable. It is an art to be learned and practiced over a period of time. The steady focus of the action process is on structures—the structures of decision and policy. The objective is to widen participation in decisions and to achieve qualitative reform of policies.

Second, social action is *deliberate* involvement. Such a change effort does not consist of a string of haphazard or routine activities that may appear useful from hindsight. Social action is planned effort to make contact with a part of the social system in order to change it. Behind such effort is the realization that the future is not determined by fate. For better or for worse, the future is formed by human activity. The actual outcome of the action may be unanticipated, but the social actionist would rather face that hazard than rely on an invisible hand to take care of his future. The actionist refuses merely to adapt to change (remembering with Rene Dubos that too much adaptation can be suicidal). The actionist intends to give change a push in a healthy direction by joining with others of mutual purpose.

However, such activism must not be confused with a sense of omnipotence, as if man could make of his world whatever he wants. Prometheus and Pandora are symbols of that futile vanity, as is the Tower of Babel. With all our modern, but fragmented, knowledge about the structure of nature and society, we have yet to learn the elementary ground rules for peaceful living, and we have only begun the slow process of physical and social renewal.

Third, social action is *group* effort. Participants are change agents who know that healthy social relations and human conditions are produced by people working together, not by each individual "doing his own thing." Obviously, initiative must be taken by individuals, and change efforts must make contact with established institutions. But the key to social action lies in group planning and implementation—by mutual effort, mutually agreed upon. The group, whether *ad hoc* or ongoing, supports action-minded individuals and provides connective links between individuals and institutions. Action groups can exert influence much more effectively than can individuals going it alone. Groups can collaborate with other groups. Groups can gather more resources. Groups have the power to develop structure by which they can change structures.

Inevitably, this puts us in the arena of politics. Broadly

conceived, politics is all that people do to build human community and to participate in its governance. Politics is a complex reality. The formal, and most frequently news-making, part of politics goes on in the legislative halls, executive offices, and judicial chambers of government. But a lot of politics also goes on in the "private" structures of society, where each sector or institution has its own form of governance and policy choices to make. This might be called informal politics. Social action is involved with both formal and informal politics. Occasionally it also spills over into electoral politics, though social action groups generally avoid direct participation in partisan campaigns. Social action focuses on influencing the policy-making process, whoever is in office. (The social action discussed here does not refer to the activities of highly or-ganized lobbies or corporate interest groups, which also work for changes in public policy. Sophisticated social ac-tion by voluntary groups often seeks to counteract the influence of these special interests.)

Effective participation in any political decision must be achieved by organized effort. And organized effort, to be effective, requires some exercise of power. Power is the capacity to overcome at least some of the resistance to a desired change. Power is an inevitable feature of social structures, though the intensity varies and there are vari-ous kinds of power to apply (crunching force being one of the least effective kinds of power in the long run). Group power is the name of the game because public policies and institutional practices tend to continue un-changed until impeded or deflected by pressures for change. So, "change power" must be gathered and exer-cised by social action groups. In this regard there is no place for shyness, but there is plenty of room for sophisti-cation.

Fourth, social action concentrates on changing *structures,* rather than relying on individual conversions. This approach abandons the popular assumption that if only enough individuals are changed, social problems will eventually be solved. The fact is that changed individuals do not necessarily change structures (though personal reorientation, of course, is desirable). People with new lifestyles who have entered large corporations are learning this hard truth. The sum of good men does *not* necessarily make good systems, no matter how well-intentioned the individuals. Corporate entities (both public and private) often hurt people and proceed mercilessly to fulfill the logic of their enterprise. Harrison Brown illustrated the point in *The New York Times Book Review* (May 24, 1970) with reference to the Military-Industrial-Academic Complex:

Few of the individuals in the system are other than men of good will. Evil thoughts and actions play little if any role in the emergence of the complex. It came into being largely because of a combination of provincialism, organizational patriotism, fear, enthusiasm, ignorance, the desire to get elected, and the desire to make a dollar, all blended in just the right proportions to produce the most dangerous and evil organism ever created by man.

Precisely because systems tend to magnify the sins of individuals, social actionists must concentrate attention on corporate practices. Personal ethics are also important, but they are not the primary focus of the social change effort.

The significance of decisions that most individuals can make tends to pale in comparison with the significance of policies set by business, industry, and government. The familiar proposition that corporate behavior is merely a collection of individual actions is only part of the truth. It is just as accurate to observe that corporate systems run the people related to them. Systems have a logic and a will of their own which set value priorities and restrict individual choice. People who do not organize to channel or resist the pressures of corporate entities have little change power.

Consider, for example, what it takes to halt and reverse the process of environmental deterioration. Individuals who change their daily routines and habits of consumption will make a cumulative difference, not only in reducing the amount of refuse, but also in cultivating new consciousness. However, the pollution of water and air is attributable, for the most part, to the activities and output of industries, utilities, developers, growers, and governmental agencies.

As Barry Commoner has shown in his book *The Closing Circle,* the 200 to 2,000 percent rise in pollution levels since 1946 cannot be attributed to growing population and affluence per se. The kinds of goods produced, and the toxic technologies involved in their production or use, account for the poisoning of the environment. And where are the decisions made about new product development and systems of production? Obviously not primarily in the average living room but in the corporate boardroom.

Environmental degradation largely results from the introduction of new industrial and agricultural production technologies. These technologies are ecologically faulty because they are designed to solve singular, separate problems and fail to take into account the inevitable "side-effects" that arise because, in nature, no part is isolated from the whole ecological fabric. . . .

The environmental crisis is the legacy of our unwitting assault on the natural systems that support us. It represents hidden costs that are mounting toward catastrophe. If it is to be resolved, these costs must be made explicit and balanced against the benefits of technology in open, public debate. But this debate will not come easily. For the public has little access to the necessary scientific data. Much of the needed information has been, and remains, wrapped in government and industrial secrecy.[10]

Commoner urges a partnership between scientists and citizens in public action on environmental issues.

Reversing the pattern of environmental deterioration depends primarily on effective mechanisms of public control, so that corporate enterprises become truly accountable to the citizens for their environmental impact. The prevailing pattern of corporate protectionism on the part of government must be altered through social action. Citizens groups can demand that companies invest a significant percent of profits in pollution prevention and publish "cycle" profiles on all chemicals and gases so we know where they come from, where they go, and who is exposed. Government needs to be pushed beyond narrow programs of cleanup, to enforce existing laws with emphasis on whole ecological systems, and to eliminate loopholes where they exist. As Ralph Nader warned in an interview with *National Wildlife* (June–July, 1971):

There are going to be serious genetic consequences and serious health consequences in this country if we fail within the next 20 years to make contamination of the environment a crime, a crime with serious penalties.

Corporate behavior (public and private) that rapes the land, befouls air and water, or creates toxic products is no longer tolerable. Of course, individuals must also change life-styles in order to protect and renew the environment. But life-styles follow technologies, and the development of technologies is determined by corporate entities. The choices they offer consumers turn out to be crucial. Thus, the environmental crisis clearly poses the need for more people to influence in organized ways the economic and political decision-making structures.

This exposes a *fifth* point regarding our definition of social action. We are interested in altering *both local community structures and major societal structures,* which are increasingly interlocked. Movement in one structure impinges on many others. An effort to change one part of society quickly affects other parts. But we are only beginning to discern the connections. All of us need to get clearer pictures of how the political and economic structures of our society mesh and where they are open to influence, infiltration, or intervention.

Social action often begins with the probing and monitoring of a public policy on the local scene. But those who stay with an issue for any length of time soon learn that many strings are pulled from outside the local community. Therefore the social action group must extend its contacts to discover where the corporate action is. This is what separates the influencers from the dilettantes.

Appropriate settings for social action are as fluid as the life-style most of us experience. (Would that we had the political education to match the opportunities of the new life-style.) Few of us live in autonomous, isolated settlements. Community and settlement are no longer equivalent for us, as they were to the residents of the ancient Greek city-state, or the medieval town, or the colonial village. Our community is less tied to place and more related to a shifting combination of interests. The kind of community we typically experience today actually consists of a plural set of subcommunities and organizational relationships involving a variety of roles and responsibilities. We experience rapid mobility and extensive contacts according to our interests in work, leisure, education, even religion.

Why not also conduct our social action at several levels and in diverse settings? We already find ourselves in a variety of structures, any of which can become arenas or channels of social action.

Those who intend to help make significant alterations in social structures will not be satisfied to remain disconnected, nor will they simply plug in where the system's managers say O.K. They will be open to a variety of fresh organizational opportunities both locally and beyond. They will not buy the notion that local action where they reside is all that matters or is manageable. *Unfortunately, many discouraged activists have abandoned the larger organizational field* where metropolitan, state, even national policies are changed, to concentrate on the immediate neighborhood or the small communal experience. Too often this approach is parochial and nostalgic, rather than politically realistic.

After all, it's an organization world. Organizations are both vehicles and obstacles to constructive change. Organizations shape the conditions in which we live and the choices we make daily. If we want to influence these conditions and choices too, then we must mobilize resources, assert goals, and build structures that challenge established institutional habits and governmental priorities. Change agents know it is necessary to intervene corporately in order to affect the corporate practices of our society.

Now some people are overwhelmed at the thought of

trying to make a corporate difference. "What can I or we do about the policies of General Motors?" Thinking about corporate action on this scale does tend to heighten a sense of impotence. But corporate action is not necessarily a large-scale effort; it is basically a matter of dealing with institutions or corporate entities where we are—working, buying, supporting, belonging, serving. The mobility and diversity of modern community is an asset in this regard. Many persons find themselves in small or larger corporate settings where it is possible to take some group initiatives for change. These structures can be affected even by a small percentage of people organized to achieve reforms, and who are linked to similar initiatives in other structures.

Sixth, the goal of social action is the *common good.* This, of course, is a rather general proposition with which most people would agree. Or at least few would admit that they are disinterested in the common good. Shortly we will consider what values should have priority when one refers to the common good. But the flexibility of the term invites a prior observation.

Efforts to alter chunks of the system or to change particular policies can serve many different ends. These objectives are defined by group interests, and our society includes a multiplicity of groups with quite diverse change goals, all being pursued in the name of peace, liberty, or equality. Appearances often obscure real diversity—for example, among the young. Some are involved in "greening" America over against the Corporate State, others are eager to become technocrats (what Peter Berger calls the "blueing" of America), and many more simply reflect the "jeaning" of America in conformity to prevailing clothing habits.

Few opinion makers, including public officials, have

caught up with the fact that activists are to be found across the political spectrum—left, center, and right. Activists are not only "leftist or liberal," nor are they to be found only among the young or the economically less advantaged. Numerous super-patriotic groups on the far right and their spokesmen (including some powerful politicians) inspire citizen activism that can be as vigorous as anything the leftward "radical" movements produce. But the "right" habitually paints the "left" as anarchic and carping, while pretending that it, the right, is orderly and supportive. This despite the fact that the far right has always been repressive of civil liberties and prone to violence, with a record of shootings and bombings that outstrips the left.

Once we cut through the stereotypes, it becomes clear that *almost any group can be sometimes militant, sometimes moderate;* and that activism is simply part of the process of fighting for social causes. Disciplined activism in the free espousal of social ideas is far preferable to silent acceptance of the *status quo.*

The social action game has been and is being played by groups of people across the entire left-center-right spectrum. It can involve a community organization of relatively poor people, a middle-class association, or a group of corporate executives. The usual difference is that the activism of the poor tends to be abrasive and confrontational because such low-power groups must clamor for attention to their grievances by every means at their disposal. (A lot of middle-class people are beginning to feel the same way.) On the other hand, the holders and beneficiaries of corporate power tend to proceed rather quietly within the rules of the system, as long as things are clearly in their control. It should be remembered that such "low-profile activism" can have drastic social effects and is capable of

suppressing protest by rewriting the rules of the system
wherever it is being challenged.

A parabolic example will help to clarify the point. The
story is paraphrased from a late summer, 1971, newspaper
account.

One hot day, a school bus loaded with black children from a
nearby East Coast city appeared at a private beach "owned" by
an exclusive association of white summer residents. The children had been romping on the beach for only a few minutes
when a patrolman working for the association told them to
leave. Middle-aged and elderly people also shouted and glared
at the intruders. Soon the police arrived. The group's leader,
a staff worker for the urban revitalization corps from the city
where the children originated, argued and pleaded to let them
stay for the day, but to no avail. Just as the disappointed children were climbing back onto the bus, a small, quiet lady
who had spent summers on the beach since her childhood
spotted the group and invited all eighty visitors to be her
guests overnight. This met the legal requirement that only
residents and their guests could use the beach. Neighbors
pressed close to try to change her mind, but she held firm. "I
can't understand this fear. Families here ought to meet some
of these children."

Meanwhile, the staff was busy persuading residents on the
beach or at their cottages to let a black child or two stay with
them overnight. Sixty were placed, but twenty had to go to a
nearby hotel. "I don't like your tactics at all," one of the residents snapped. "Rather than being forced into this, I'd prefer
to offer." The leader replied that a formal request to the
association would have produced a polite turnaway. Another
resident, a lawyer who took in two seven-year-old girls, observed: "A lot of people who say this thing should be voluntary, wouldn't volunteer if given the opportunity. I wouldn't
have done anything unless confronted with this immediate
choice."

Whether such a beaching program actually softened racial prejudice is uncertain. The children of both races, with few exceptions, were quite friendly. But the cold reaction of many adults spoiled the day for some of the visitors who could barely hide their hurt. Subsequently, the association lodged a formal complaint about the "invasion" with the city council and refused to meet with the group leader to clear the air. The city council decided to bar all busloads of children in the future unless it could be shown that each child had a resident sponsor. A statewide legal issue may develop from this incident.

Note that the low-power group had few options but to confront the people who were withholding the resources. But the association which "owned" the beach quietly proceeded to rewrite the rules in hopes that they would not have to share the beach. The incident exposes a struggle between groups over a structure, as well as a very personal issue involving immediate choice, shaped by the initiative of a few individuals. The incident is also a poignant reminder of the difficulties attendant upon trying to achieve the common good.

One crucial test of the common good is the probable effect of any policy on the "little people," the low-power groups, the under-represented. One does not have social justice where the interests of the disadvantaged are ignored. An obvious model is to be found in the struggle for racial equality. What is the primary responsibility of the Establishment (government, business, educational institutions, churches, social facilities) as whites react to the minority push for shared decision-making power, economic opportunity, and adequate education and housing? A proper definition of the common good would rule out any compromise of minority rights in the face of white anxiety because the relative inconvenience experienced by some of the majority hardly compares with the miserable conditions into which most of the racial minorities have been forced.

So the common good means fairness (or justice) to each, as defined by the self-evident truth "that all men are created equal, that they are endowed by their Creator with certain unalienable Rights, that among these are Life, Liberty, and the pursuit of Happiness.—That to secure these rights, Governments are instituted among Men, deriving their just powers from the consent of the governed." Incidentally, the next sentence of this familiar text (the Declaration of Independence) is a credo for vigorous social action. "That whenever any Form of Government [read 'any corporate leadership'] becomes destructive of these ends, it is the Right of the People to alter or abolish it, and to institute new Government . . . to effect their Safety and Happiness."

This is a clear political definition of the common good, with the emphasis on justice. To it should be related another moral value—the hope of reconciliation between people and groups. The goal of social action is to demonstrate the meaning of justice and reconciliation in the public-policy arena. The primary aim is to create structures for equitable sharing of power and resources. This struggle is humanized, i.e., the action takes on compassionate qualities when it is informed by the overarching norm of reconciliation. People who grasp the meaning of reconciliation recognize the creation of one human race, having diverse cultures, but sharing a common historical destiny. People can unite in caring for mutual long-run interests.

An expectation of reconciliation makes all the difference

in the struggle for justice. This does not terminate conflict nor make it avoidable; rather, conflict occurs in the light of an awareness of the larger human community. This provides a framework for limiting "warfare" over social issues and encourages a search for policies that serve the general welfare. As I put the matter in another book, *Reconciliation and Conflict:* "Reconciliation is the direction of the political quest for economic well-being, peace among nations, and social equality." Reconciliation is the fundamental norm for evaluating what is going on in social relations. It is the clue to personal growth and the transformation of institutional structures. Those who anticipate this renewal of human community must expect, and can live freely with, conflict. "Reconciliation leads to and through conflict. . . . Reconciliation gives conflict limited character and a positive purpose. No conflict is ultimate, nor can it claim final allegiance from men who grasp the freedom to be human and who seek the humanization of society." [11] With this perspective we are "freed up" to work for equality of conditions and quality of life, including the empowerment of those who lack the means to achieve a decent livelihood, and who also want their children to survive and be educated, and to pursue happiness.

3

SOME RELATED ACTIVITIES

Social action as defined above relates to, but is distinct from, several other activities. A brief review of these related activities may help to avoid confusion.

Social Education

In an educational context persons are informed about social issues or problems (and have their public conscience formed). The informing can occur by means of classroom instruction, reading, speeches, rallies, forums, investigative journalism, and the use of a wide range of study materials. Social education also takes place through intergroup encounters, go-and-see experiences, and such mechanisms as simulation games or short-term internships. These modes of "involvement education" can be quite activating. But one should not assume that participation in educational events is likely to lead to automatic implementation of the learning. Action does not necessarily grow out of knowing—study, awareness, understanding. (If that were so, why is there so much material written about social issues as compared to the amount of citizen action which takes place?) Sometimes analysis only leads to paralysis, as the author knows firsthand.

But the above paragraph is *not* intended to downgrade the value of social education. Knowledge is necessary if action is to be wise. People need to encounter social reality, including exposure to outspoken advocates and opponents of new policies. They also need to face hard facts and to experience the disciplines of rational discourse, and issue analysis, as well as to learn tolerance for contradictory viewpoints. Progressive civil life is more likely to flourish wherever such virtues are practiced.

Yet much education is unfocused, and therefore relatively ineffective. Social education becomes more effective when it is oriented to the achievement of concrete action goals. People who have decided to do something about a particular community or societal condition have a readiness to explore the problem in detail. Such education is purposive.

For example, when a group decides to push for programs to combat hunger in America, the group has to begin looking at structural causes of the lack of food, sources of official foot-dragging, uneven pricing policies of business, and the inadequacy of existing delivery systems such as food stamps and free school lunches. In 1969, a coalition of national organizations including several church groups, collaborating with the National Council of Negro Women, set out to eradicate hunger through the establishment of better food distribution procedures and advocacy of a guaranteed income to meet the long-range problem. This ambitious action goal was pursued by direct participation in the December, 1969, White House Conference on Food, Nutrition, and Health, and then by widespread planning for community action. The local groups were pushed to educate themselves by asking: Where are the poor and hungry in this area? What is the welfare program and food program in this county? How are these public services administered? What is Congress doing, or not doing, about minimum standards and funding?

Being clear about action needs and at least some tentative policy objectives makes for lively learning. Learners are delivered from the illusion that they can wait to obtain "the facts" from all sides before entertaining an action goal. Setting aside the rationalistic bias (i.e., reliance on knowledge to produce action), the actionist points to man's intentional nature (the crucial role of social willpower). Man brings purpose to each set of facts, in much the same way that the computer he programs does. He explores facts from one point of view and he tends to ignore many operational considerations until he establishes an action objective.

Given these realities, there is promise in the action-reflection model of education. Consciousness grows in the process of exploring an agreed-upon task. Some educators might contend that this approach prematurely reduces the area of exploration. But these days our senses are numbed, and our information-processing mechanisms are overloaded by a host of issues and facts. Is it not both more practical and sane to let the education follow the action desire, and to concentrate educationally on selected issues for a time?

Education should be evaluated in terms of freeing people to act. It should be designed to help people work within and upon social institutions for the public good.

Social Service

Many of those who are most involved in voluntary organizations, including churches, seem to have difficulty making a distinction between social service and social action. They want to help meet the needs of the disadvantaged, and they usually identify an opportunity in terms of supporting a community service. This is characteristic of civic groups, United Fund organizations, the federal voluntary service setup that is called "ACTION," as well as much that middle-class citizens would most naturally favor by way of social betterment.

Proponents of service projects that help to fill gaps in public services deserve citizen support. The social actionist ought *not* to deny the need for services, especially when so many public services are deteriorating. But the maintenance or improvement of community health, education, and welfare services "is *not* social action if it expresses or grows out of some already existing commitment of the community or a part of the community. Such commitments, if they are indeed established commitments, are part of the existing order." [12]

The typical purpose of a service effort is to help marginal individuals function better, so as to strengthen the existing order. Service usually deals with cases (as does the social worker) rather than with structures (as does the action leader). In general, social service organizations routinize the thrust of earlier social action movements. On the other hand, a new social action thrust often reflects the inadequacy of the present system and its public services.

Thus, public welfare services grew out of early twentieth-century protests against the unrelieved plight of disabled workers and the urban poor. Now the *functioning* of the welfare system is in question. Some social actionists have been organizing recipients into welfare-rights groups determined to end demeaning regulations and to demand a fair amount of disposable income to compensate for the lack of job opportunities. At the same time there is growing taxpayer pressure and official alarm over the increase in the size of the welfare roll. (Tragically, the rhetoric focuses on "undeserving recipients" and "work requirements," instead of on the depressed economic state of many communities and the high percentage of recipients who are under age or otherwise unable to work.)

Meanwhile others are working to devise a new structure of income maintenance that provides income grants above the Social Security Administration's "poverty level," administered according to uniform national standards, and free from mandatory work requirements. Potentially this kind of income-maintenance structure would constitute a major social reform in a country where at present nine million Americans who could qualify for welfare are not receiving it because of lack of uniform standards, inequitable administration, or refusal of potential recipients to subject themselves to indignity.

Many middle-class groups, however, are not thinking in these terms. Typically, they begin at the point of organizing assistance to individuals in need of food, shelter, health care, supplementary education, etc. This kind of relief may help temporarily, but it is often paternalistic in character and politically ineffectual because it leaves oppressive structures untouched.

Consider, for example, what it takes to make progress in the urban public education sector. Concerned voluntary organizations characteristically launch a person-to-person service effort, such as a tutoring program for inner-city children. As inspiring and personally rewarding as some of the volunteer effort might be, this activity in itself hardly begins to meet the need of massive numbers of children who will remain functionally illiterate. Unequal public education opportunity is a systemic problem requiring regional financing, community involvement, and compensatory redistribution of resources for instruction. Service projects are no substitute for structural changes of this kind.

Social action seeks to get at the sources of inequity and depression in the system. Social action groups look behind the obvious service request to examine how particular institutions and policies affect the people they are supposed to serve. It usually turns out that more of the difficulty is located in the Establishment's policies than in the problem cases. When we are faced with deteriorating public services, the appropriate action stance is to advocate restructuring or even replacing the services so that they are no longer a "disservice" to the dignity and self-development of the people to be served. In the process of pushing for major policy changes, action groups can help to expose and debunk popular illusions about the nature and sources of public problems.

Social Witness

A few veterans in the field also find it helpful to distinguish between social action and social witness. In the words of Thomas E. Price, a churchman writing in the United Methodist magazine *Engage* (January 1–15, 1971), social witness is the art of "making public, by word and/or deed, convictions of an individual, organization, or institution on particular social issues. Social witness may be individual or corporate." Its main object is to register a strong conviction or conscientious viewpoint, to take a stand.

Too often the problem with such public witness or advocacy is not that it occurs, but that it remains isolated. A strong viewpoint is expressed, but it fails to register (big voice, small stick). The stance does not fit into a larger strategy of organized group action. A typical example is to be found in petitions that are circulated for signature. When received, their stirring words are simply added to the pile.

To some extent the street demonstration shares the same fate. Often it is more ventilative of the participants' feelings than it is effective in bringing about a policy change. However, it can make quite a difference when followed up legislatively, as were some of the antiwar demonstrations of the late 1960's and 1970, which in turn were patterned on the big marches of the civil rights movement.

When social witness becomes a facet of a broader social action strategy, the situation is much more promising. Words and other deeds of witness are formulated to anticipate related action. Implementing mechanisms begin to receive explicit attention. Declarations become part of the process of action, rather than a substitute for it.

One additional comment is in order on the subject of resolutions and public statements. Many activists have begun to denigrate words in favor of deeds. This is a rather thoughtless dichotomy. Words, after all, are deeds. Words are very important to the social action scene. Without carefully formulated words, there would be no coherent definition of issues, no compelling advocacy of better policies. But this is not to recommend merely hurling words out there somewhere in the hope that someone will heed them. Just as social actionists have begun to recognize the need for more focused education, so they have also learned that it is necessary to back up any public witness with an organized constituency and a strategic use of resources.

Although we have noted the distinctions between action, education, service, and witness, it would be unfortunate to conclude that the distinctions are essential in all circumstances. *These forms of social involvement are actually closely interrelated.* The distinctions help us to sort out what emphasis we will give to these functions and to avoid being distracted from the action agenda. People who take social action seriously will influence also these other forms of involvement. Thus, if one were to compare contemporary approaches to social action behavior with approaches that prevailed more than a decade ago, or even a few years ago, one would find that today's actors are less sanguine about the effectiveness of general social education, more alert to paternalism in social services, less satisfied to leave the action at the level of momentary public witness.

If this and the previous chapter help to clarify the social action task, then their purpose is fulfilled. However, we should not move on without noting the difficulty of the task. When it comes to social action, we face a paradox. The task is left to volunteers, but it demands know-how and imagination—all the more so as involvement deepens. I agree with George Crowell that

few activities in our society, even among our socially prescribed obligations [job and family], are more demanding than is the task of initiating social action. . . . It requires intelligence in order that social issues, whose ramifications can be overwhelmingly complex, may be clearly understood. It requires a willingness to work without immediate achievement of goals, and without promise of favorable recognition. And, indeed, it requires a willingness to risk opposition and disapproval.[13]

Pondering these difficulties, one might conclude that the prospects for effective social action are far from promising, even that they are dismal. But there is evidence of a new determination to change institutional practices and social structures. People *are* showing the initiative to help construct a future, rather than merely resigning themselves within their respective roles to the course of events. Those who make the required effort will find few limitations on their involvement. But it takes discipline as well as some weekends.

4

RADICAL ENDS, REALISTIC MEANS

The social action process includes both what and how, both vision and know-how, both ends and means. Its purpose is to participate in a qualitative renewal of social structures. While this kind of activism can go in any direction, it should be disciplined by a fresh understanding of what it takes to get justice and reconciliation in contemporary society. Therefore, this chapter proposes a particular approach to social action featuring radical perspective and realistic technique. (If the word "radical" miscarries, try "reconstructive.")

A realistically radical approach to social action is, we hope, an advance over the stylized approaches of the late '60s. During the '60s many public officials and social action leaders were ambivalent about objectives and pre-occupied with style. The preoccupation with style at the expense of substance went far beyond the presidential behavior of John Kennedy, who called for a New Frontier, or Richard Nixon, who at least tried out the notion of a New American Revolution (soon displaced by the New Economic Policy, etc.). While both Presidents projected more newness than they produced, the latter's call for a New American Revolution was especially incongruous, coming as it did from the leading antirevolutionary of the '60s who, after stridently attacking young radicals and their supporters, tried to co-opt their rhetoric for purposes of reshuffling the federal bureaucracy.

Perhaps the preoccupation with style was fitting irony in an era in which the major prophecy was, "The medium is the message" (Marshall McLuhan). *Style itself became strategy as did the corresponding anti-style.* The characteristic action style of the dissenters on the Left was to undertake mass demonstrations and particularly to occupy or disrupt symbolic locations of the System's "dirty work." The typical anti-style of the resenters on the Right was to denounce "violent protest," and to demand obedient respect for the American way. People were playing with distorted images right and left. We could hardly get away from stereotypes of social action and civil disobedience.

The actual pattern of social ferment did not fit the stereotypes. There was a noticeable increase in spectacular *witness,* but not much follow-up *action.* Large segments of the public were led to believe that the country's existence was immediately threatened by widespread anarchy. But the bulk of all the protest activity was legally within bounds delineated by the Bill of Rights. Meanwhile, those heated disputes about style distracted us from sustained efforts to meet public needs. There was little progress toward terminating institutional racism, redesigning foreign policy, stopping the arms race, overcoming hunger and poverty, building quality of life. Much more time was spent measuring and manipulating feelings about disorder. One result was a measurable increase in governmental efforts to curtail the exercise of civil liberties.

Of course, some of the protest styles did help to dramatize stubborn social need. The intention was to awaken the Mute Majority out of its studied apathy. But the majority became aroused mostly about the behavior of the militant minority and the minority was soon preoccupied with repressive police measures. As though they were dealing with a spectator sport, people were asked to choose whether they were for the aggregation of Revolters or for the Establishment forces. The Mute Majority supported repression of dissent and ignored the logical outcome— that out of authoritarian pacification comes violent insurgency. Meanwhile, few people were mobilized to undertake sustained action.

Even so, there were civil rights gains and some belated results from the opposition to the Vietnam war. Most of this was due not to spectacular protest or high-octane rhetoric, but to patient organization on the part of small segments of the public. The people who were serious about social action knew that dramatic confrontation is to sociopolitical action as heated argument is to marriage. It brings things into focus, but too much time spent at it is likely to fracture the situation. In a healthy marriage the partners spend time doing what is mutually beneficial. The style is usually unspectacular; many of the tasks are even humdrum. Similarly, in the case of social action, effectiveness consists primarily of creative planning and patient organization, with relatively little emphasis on spectacular deeds or rhetoric.

Stylistic diversity remains, of course, and it can be appreciated. To take a prominent example, some social actionists describe their task as *revolution.* They think in terms of big leaps or drastic changes in the system. Others talk in terms of *reform.* They envision more modest revisions of public policy and institutional practice. But whether persons believe in revolution or reform, *what they do to meet specific issues may not be so different.* Similar elements of action discipline and, often, a commonality of effort can be seen across the revolution-reform split. One begins to discern a similar agenda more basic than the difference in vocabulary.

The task we share is to seek radical ends by realistic means. Whether one tunes in the National Urban Coalition, Friends of the Earth, or Common Cause; Saul Alinsky, or Carl Ogelsby; the National Student Association, the National Association for the Advancement of Colored People, or the National Women's Political Caucus; a black power convention or the United Farm Workers Organizing Committee; a major church assembly, a mayor's conference, or a professional association; James Reston, C. Eric Lincoln, Charles Reich, or Peter Berger—the message has a similar motif: Seek basic reform by action pressure; bring off qualitative alterations of the system.

Radical Ends

The goal is to achieve a basic reorientation of the society. To expect this via present structures and leadership as such is naïve, but to hope for change via apocalyptic revolution is pathetic. In other words it is wrong simply to perpetuate the belief that plenty of change can be had if you just play by the rules of the existing system. The existing order and its rules have been too restrictive, unresponsive, even repressive. But it is just as wrong to cultivate romantic notions about bringing down the system via guerrilla assaults and then starting from scratch. Bland assurance, heady talk—neither approach nurtures social action maturity.

Fundamental reform motivated by radical consciousness and pursued by realistic means promises better results. Before the reader dismisses this orientation, he should ponder the available options and weigh their prospects. The other available options are: (*a*) to try to keep the system as it is, running in place but deteriorating; (*b*) to seek radical ends by radical means, which escalates toward terrorism or a military coup; or (*c*) to pursue moderate ends by radical means, which produces revolutionary posturing. In other words, we are thinking in terms of evolutionary mutations, not violent revolution. Both something old and something new inform this radical-and-realistic approach.

The new factor, which is not new in history but which is unfamiliar to many North Americans, can be identified as a *radical consciousness* that the social system itself must be changed fundamentally. Not just tinkered with, or torn up, but transformed. "Radicalization is the process of looking afresh at the institutions and procedures of the society, beginning with their roots and working onward, taking nothing for granted or as being of continuing value except these indispensible things: community, self-rule, the integrity of the human person, and the necessity of living in harmony with the natural order." [14] The objective of the new social consciousness is to change fundamentally all the conditions that cripple these essential aims.

Radicalization means thinking big about basic value priorities. The radical vision of society generates a commitment to build alternative institutional structures that produce *both* quality of life and equality of opportunity. Each segment of the population that is gripped by this vision gives it a slightly different emphasis, depending on the details of the situation each group faces and its sense of cultural heritage, but the consciousness itself is widely shared.

For some, the experience of new social consciousness is not particularly intense—it is just a growing awareness of the chasm between democratic creed and human need, or a restlessness about unresponsive and unimaginative public policies. It is a conviction that basic reforms must be made now. People having this conviction may not perceive themselves as radical, since that term has "wild" connotations and they are seeking to extend classic political values such as liberty, justice, general welfare, and security. But if "radical" means to implement "root" values, then these values are radical. (*Liberty* is the ability to choose, shape, and implement one's own thoughts and actions. *Justice* has to do with equality in law, fair administration of policy, and widespread intergroup respect. *General Welfare* refers to a state of happiness resulting from the fulfillment of health, education, and subsistence needs. And *Security* is the absence of threat to the existence of community life, without which domestic tranquillity becomes impossible.)

For others the new consciousness begins with "seeing the light." Perhaps a flash of social insight occurs as one struggles over dissonant facts such as the gross military budget and the arsenal of a nation that professes to be peaceful, while staggering numbers of her children and elderly live in poverty. Why let it happen? Or, perhaps, one is radicalized by encountering dissenters who have been singled out for punishment by government or another institution.

The "new" consciousness is more outraged by intolerable social conditions, more demanding of fundamental human rights, more insistent on basic (systemic) change. It is strong among the racially excluded, the economically deprived, and educated youth, but it crosses generational, geographical, and organizational barriers. Today's seekers of fundamental social change are grappling with analytical and action paradigms that expose the incoherence of the present system, expose new possibilities for human relationships, and seek different forms of power and social structure shaped toward humane ends. The radically conscious feel and celebrate a newfound freedom to pursue those life-styles, to combat those evils, and to build those counter-institutions which they did not previously dare to attempt. The evils to be combated include racism, imperialism, and corporate indifference.

Emerging counter-institutions can vary all the way from communal families to war-resistance groups, to economic cooperatives, to free schools, to new political alliances, to separate structures of minority group self-development. The new is being planned and built amid styles and institutions that may not yet be dead, but are perceived as hollow. This is the nature of a revolution *within* society, a great awakening. It is a process of parallel development, of displacement without widespread destruction, of letting the decay of the old institutions take its course.

Realistic Means

But the problem remains of precisely what to do and how to do it effectively. Movements of radical consciousness seldom pursue these questions in practical terms, since they are so painfully aware of the failures of society, so immediately visionary about the world as they would like it to be, and only marginally related to people who hold institutional power. This posture does not leave much time for inquiry about, or manipulation of, the mechanisms of change. That practical task is left to organizations that are working to achieve specific social-policy goals. They have to determine and take concrete steps to change particular chunks of the system. These action organizations intend to get results, not to swap revelations. As Saul Alinsky, the dean of community organizers, observes, working for specific results is "the difference between being a realistic radical and being a rhetorical one."

Alinsky likens effective organization for change to a three-act play: "The first act introduces the characters and the plot, in the second act the plot and characters are developed as the play strives to hold the audience's attention. In the final act good and evil have their confrontation and resolution. The present generation wants to go right into the third act, skipping the first two, in which case there is no play, nothing but confrontation for confrontation's sake—a flare-up and back to darkness. To build a powerful organization takes time." [15]

Realistic methods of action require patience. Careful attention must be paid to the actual setup and the interests of the people involved. Until a unity of interest and commitment is uncovered and practical action channels are identified, the effort of any group to produce change remains unrealistic.

Above all, the social actionist needs a sober understanding of power, its locations, kinds, and uses. Power comes into play whenever there is contention over any question of policy. Power is a neutral means—it can be used for purposes of institutional foot-dragging or to apply pressure for change. It can be exercised destructively or constructively. But the power to decide or influence policy is not neutral. The lack of such power is a structural cause of injustice. Precisely because power tempts those who use it to act unjustly toward others, the realist knows that power is best handled by sharing it. This applies to the internal life of organizations as well as to the relationships of groups in the larger society.

Several additional observations need to be made about the realism recommended here, lest it be misunderstood. For just as radical consciousness has misleading advocates, so does realism about methods of action. The characteristic failing of the "realist" is to seek too little, to compromise too quickly with things as they are. The realistic radical has a different mind-set.[16]

1. *The realistic radical is guided by concern for the powerless.* Powerless means having relatively less power than most people. (One does not have to be poor to be powerless.) Injustice occurs to those who lack power. Therefore, powerlessness must be overcome. Unfortunately, many who call themselves realists have gone down a different road. They might better be called "impaled rationalizers," for those in power who, caught on the horns of each new dilemma, imply that little can be done. The rationalizers are so preoccupied with the sinfulness of men and the ambiguity of causes that they have no big change goals. They view bad situations as necessary for the sake of social order. Almost anything from MIRV warheads to minority oppression can be rationalized that way, especially if the realist fancies himself as playing the role of major policy maker.

Such determinism has nothing to do with the perspective of the realistic radical. He is alert first of all not to the reasons policy makers give for the existing situation, but to the injustice experienced by the most powerless. The plight of the system's victims or rejects provides his clue to reality. From it he begins to draw parallels to his own experience of political impotence and in it he looks for linkages among the powerless.

2. *The realistic radical accepts the need for forceful*

social action. He knows that powerful people and organizations are insulated, even selfish, in their decision-making. They must be pushed to serve the common good, even though they always claim to be serving it and never admit to having been pushed. Actually, public officials tend to postpone enlightened policy moves until they are forced to make them. And often they must be stimulated again to implement policies vigorously and equitably. To obtain more than cheap policy promises, social action groups must exercise persuasive or coercive power. Call it *push power.*

Sometimes the use of push power reaches the point of violating accepted rules of behavior. However, the realistic radical will resist the tendency of the last generation's realists to concentrate their criticism on the behavior of protestors. The behavior of the powerful deserves more criticism than that of the powerless, for the simple reason that the powerful can do more to change conditions, and in resisting, do more damage to the common life, even if by covert means.

High-power groups by their very nature do not need to undertake direct action—demonstrations, strikes, boycotts, civil disobedience, or threat of disruption. Privileged groups can accept or resist change rather quietly. High-power groups can work their will by means of influence and deployment of resources within the accepted (or newly rewritten) rules. *Low-power* groups must clamor for public attention and a share of the society's benefits by abrasive means. Much depends on the responsiveness of current institutional leadership when faced with disruptive pressures from low-power groups seeking basic reforms.

3. Still, *the realistic radical tries to act by just means.* Just causes have little chance of becoming established

policies unless they are justly sought. This stance is partly pragmatic, since radical movements and action groups are vulnerable more for their tactics than for their visions. But adherence to just means of action also follows from an intrinsic moral consideration—namely, that people should act in proportion to the evil being combated and in patterns they would want universalized. Here we sense the socio-political significance of the golden rule. We must consider what particular actions mean not only to us, but to all who experience and observe our action.

The reference to "just means" is a deliberate reminder of a tradition of moral thought that may help us to think through our responsibility in situations of public and in-stitutional conflict, such as occur in the social action process. The good to be accomplished by any action strategy must be greater than the harm it is likely to inflict. Also the strategy should have a reasonable chance of success. And the action effort must clearly reflect inten-tions for the common good. Action groups should proceed through lawfully established channels and undertake to a minimal extent possibly illegal measures, avoiding violence to persons (and to property insofar as possible). Violent insurgency becomes a last resort, *in extremis*. In other words, the means must be discriminate about the target of action, proportionate to the end-in-view, and designed to revitalize community, rather than to obliterate opposing groups of people.

4. *The realistic radical avoids excessive use of one tactic.* He knows that a mix of tactics makes for creative social action on the part of his group or organization. He wants to keep his options open, so that he can do the un-expected. He does not want to be typed as either militant or moderate. The extremist, by contrast, espouses and

pursues one action methodology, excluding all others. The extremist insists on one style . . . or else! This tendency is not limited to the lunatic fringe; it is also prominent among self-styled moderates who are prompted by every incident to define appropriate public behavior. The realistic radical will beware of both the rhetorical revolutionary and the extremist of the center or right.

The main point is to avoid locking oneself into action styles that are currently fashionable, whether daring or noncontroversial. Creative controversy should occur as part of the social action process. There is no simple definition of what behavior is legitimate and what behavior doesn't fit. Certainly, there will be little constructive change without friction, conflict, risk. Therefore, depending upon the groups and grievances involved, appropriate methods of action can include techniques of persuasion and influence, cooperation and noncooperation, advocacy and opposition, and such methods as symbolic expression, lawsuits, mass presences, coalitions of interest, proxy tactics, boycotts, strikes, and civil disobedience.

5. *The realistic radical works with existing situations.* He does not wait for a utopian setup before he enters into action. He knows that radical consciousness can become so impatient with things as they are that alienation, not action, results. The realistic radical does not expect unjust social structures to collapse at the first exposé or sound of protest. But he also avoids the temptation to accept things as they are. To work with existing situations is not to endorse them. It means to *start* where groups and issues are, with firm convictions about the direction in which they ought to be pushed. Instead of assuming that the situation is unstructured, or unorganized, the realistic radical will look for the patterns and groups already opera-

tive. He will concentrate on participating in groups that show promise of clarifying key issues and developing new vision.

6. *The realistic radical is open to new perceptions of reality.* He does not assume that the situation is neatly defined and the big questions already settled, merely waiting for implementation. His picture of what the times demand is reformable. As a participant in the new consciousness, he expects to revise his definition of the situation and his action plans in the light of significant events and changing conditions where he is. He continually reexamines what *is* happening, and what *ought* to be done next, as well as *how* to influence the outcome. By all means his action vision should be insistent, for there is a human urgency about the struggle over social priorities and public policies.

The wanted alterations will not take place merely through adjustment or liberalization of political or social opinion. Society must teach itself wholly new values, accept major new additions to its old declarations of blessedness, viz.:

Blessed are those who interrupt, for practically everything now ongoing can profit from derailment or bad bumps.

Blessed is the sense of Possibility, for it is the prime energy-source of men who interrupt.

Blessed is Openness (open personalities, open classrooms, openness to experience in the large), for it alone protects interrupters from falling into habit and passivity of their own.[17]

5

STRATEGIC THINKING

Strategic thinking is the crux of effective social involvement. Strategic thinking can be defined as disciplined, imaginative planning for action to meet a conscious imperative. The definition is broad, to counteract a constricted view of strategy. In recent years social action thought has gone flat at the point of strategizing. Strategy has become mechanical, technique-oriented, too easily identified with mere how-to-do-it questions. But the *how*-to is unimportant if the *what*-to is insignificant. Conversely, the *what* remains undeveloped if the *how* is unexplored.

More attention, then, needs to be directed to the full range of strategic thinking (which also encompasses ethical and operational thought), instead of jumping immediately into questions of tactics. To avoid reinforcing that habit, I have saved a discussion of tactics for the next chapter. I do not contend that strategy is unrelated to tactics. I only emphasize that tactics are a part, but not the whole, of strategy.

According to the early nineteenth-century military scientist Karl von Clausewitz, strategy is the theory of the use of battles for the conduct of war; tactics involve the theory of the use of forces in battle. The terms apply metaphorically to the principles or rationale underlying sociopolitical action. Thus, action tactics refer to specific moves of political "forces" against and with other forces in concrete situations. Action strategy is the use of tactical moves to approach basic social objectives or ideological goals.

Strategy corresponds to policy-making; tactics correspond to situational maneuvering. To take a familiar example, from 1969 to 1971, various groups in the peace movement, which sought a complete U.S. pullout from Vietnam, saw that public sentiment was finally swinging in their direction. What maneuvers would be most appropriate to gain the strategic objective of a prompt end to all aspects of U.S. involvement in the Indochina war? Was it better tactically to hold mass marches, to undertake disruptive group actions, or to mobilize support for congressional measures to "set the date"? The question was never resolved. All three approaches were tried by different groups, with rather mixed results. Furthermore, quite different meanings were attached to these tactics by their advocates and segments of the public.

This brings up two important facts of life: (1) in social action there is no accepted arbiter of strategic judgments; and (2) it is difficult to achieve large-scale collaboration in dealing with any issue. In fact, there are no precise standards, no blueprints; it all looks more like expressions of public art. And as in an art show, one compares both technique and images portrayed—the overall effect. Given such a pluralistic and fluid situation, one does not expect the millennium. But one can cultivate coherence in strategic thinking—a willingness to think through the considerations that ought to inform any action choice.

FIVE STRATEGY QUESTIONS

What follows is a deliberate oversimplification of a rich and complex subject. The formulation is my own, though hardly unique. I intend it to be useful in planning and evaluating social action efforts, as well as to stimulate more pertinent inquiry. To assist the memory, I propose that all strategic thinking divides into five parts which can be focused in question form:

1. What is the particular social problem confronting us? (Or, what needs changing?)
2. Why does this problem (issue, policy) exist? (Or, how did it arise?)
3. What should we do about it? (Or, what is the action goal?)
4. How shall we move to attain it? (Or, where are the action handles?)
5. What are the action results? (Or, how has the action altered the situation?)

Each of these questions triggers a number of considerations, as will be shown shortly. However, one preliminary caution is necessary.

Strategic thinking does not necessarily proceed in the order that these questions appear here. *Strategic thinking can begin at any of these five points.* Although the logical order is from action interest to issue exploration, to choice of objectives, to method of implementation, to evaluation of results, strategic thinking can move in other ways. It can move from implementation (question 4) to new ideas of the problem (question 1) and its origin (question 2).

This happened in a striking way in the early phases of black power militance, when whites tried to mobilize support of the movement in the white community. Despite creative forms of interpretation, inability to move white-controlled institutions rapidly toward deeds of racial justice clarified the nature and source of the problem. Primarily it turned out to be a "White Problem" reinforced by every conceivable institutional practice. We learned that white-controlled institutions are usually set up to benefit the majority at the expense of a subordinated minority. (This is the frequent result though not necessarily the conscious intention.) Separatism and inequality are white creations demanding correction by whites, in the light of minority-community grievances and by means of shared decision-making power.

The above illustration shows how strategic thinking can move from inadequate implementation to deeper analysis of the problem. While evaluating the results of an unsatisfactory action effort, we may be prompted to redefine the problem, its sources, our goals, and a new battle plan. The five strategic questions are closely interrelated because it is good common moral sense to inquire into the occasions, origins, objectives, methods, and consequences of actions.

Those who argue that the order of thought is very important would do well to ponder this ancient Taoist verse:

> A centipede was quite happy
> Until a toad in fun
> Asked it which leg came after which?
> This wrought it up to such a pitch
> It fell exhausted in a ditch
> Not knowing how to run.

There are other examples of the same malady, such as the *ordo salutis* obsession. *Ordo salutis* means order of salvation. Someone is forever insisting that salvation or well-being comes by doing "this" before "that" (e.g., seventeenth- and eighteenth-century theologians argued at length about whether one was first justified and then sanctified, or vice versa). The same thing happens in the field of social-change theory, some insisting that if you get the ideology straight, all else follows; others demanding exhaustive analysis of the problem before proposing any action point of view; still others requiring step-by-step objectives and procedures before deciding to proceed (call this last one Planner's Syndrome).

In short, don't worry if your mind jumps around instead of working straight from 1 to 5. However, it should sharpen your strategic insight to think through these questions. (We are taking up questions 1, 2, and 3 in this chapter, reserving questions 4 and 5 for the next.)

1. What is the particular social problem confronting us?

Obviously there are many specific problems or issues that might concern us, or ought to receive priority attention. But it is necessary in social action to concentrate on specific social policy questions that *confront us* where we are, that actually arouse our direct interest, or that require our action, *and* that we can envision ourselves tackling in a specific way. In other words, it becomes a social problem insofar as we have the will or the need to change a policy and find it appropriate to take part.

The definition of social problems in terms that confront us is characteristic of individuals and groups as well as of governments. At any given time, only some social needs receive public attention or are emphasized as major problems. Meanwhile, other conditions are hardly discussed or even recognized in the mainstream of society. Apparently, conditions only become problems in the sense of breaking through to public consciousness when there is a combination of the following elements: a shared need to change a given condition or policy, deliberate efforts to increase citizen awareness (which intensifies the need to act), and a legitimation of the problem by officials.[18] The problem fails to become a priority concern unless groups of people identify with the issue and a few powers-that-be give the issue some recognition.

This combination usually works for structural change, but not always in a constructive direction, as evidenced by the law-and-order campaigns of 1968 and 1970. In those circumstances, official recognition of the problem was so manipulative of citizen emotions that "crime prevention" legislation of ill-conceived kinds passed on Capitol Hill and in many statehouses. Social actionists should beware of any suddenly prominent, or overtly partisan, recognition of a social issue. Such issues lack a promising profile because they tend to polarize citizen responses, forcing either/or choices between unreasonable policy options.

Healthier social action situations develop when official recognition follows citizen initiative to meet a social need, as illustrated by the growing interest in penal reform—intensified by the slaughter at Attica. Only inadvertently have public officials exposed the plight of the imprisoned. Details of brutality and racism have been dug out gradually by enterprising investigative reporters. People are realizing that most jails and prisons are depressing, overcrowded places, dangerous to their inmates, and schools for criminality; though they are intended to protect the larger society by removing felons from circulation and "reforming" them during this time. Now there is a push—involving growing numbers of citizens groups—to re-examine the effects of imprisonment and to change the whole penal system in order to concentrate resources, not on building "new and better" facilities, but on rehabilitation *without* incarceration, especially for persons convicted of "crimes against property." Additional failures in the administration of justice are also being "discovered," such as the startling number of poor persons rotting in jails for lengthy periods while awaiting trial in courts with full dockets. A sound social action strategy brings these systemic failures to light in a way that they cannot be ignored.

Not every issue that confronts us is an appropriate priority for action because it does not raise fundamental questions of social policy, or because other matters may be more urgent. Sometimes it is better to concentrate on an emerging problem, or an unexplored aspect of an issue, rather than to commit energy to a prominent crusade. However, we do not always have the luxury of choosing our issues, or of sizing up a problem before we are forced to take action. We are "thrown" into many issues by events, by sensational public statements, by muckraking journalism, by the organized action of others. In a changing society many issues of public and institutional importance come at us. They are not sitting there waiting to be discovered. We are always being acted upon or being asked to support another's action. Yet we still have the option of paying more or less attention to the issues confronting us, of helping to redefine them, and of choosing our mode of response to them.

Discerning and defining the problem or problems that we intend to tackle is an analytical task. The analysis always occurs in a context of bias, for we ourselves are interested observers.

The analytical function can be summarized in terms of discerning *who is doing what to whom and how.* In fact, it is good discipline for the probers of an issue to state the problem in one indicative sentence. The sentence should indicate:

Who is doing (or not doing) something; *what* is being done (or not being done); to *whom* it is being done (or not being done); and *when* or *where* it is being done (or not being done).

When people settle down to writing such a sentence, they can come up with statements like this: "The ten suburbs of Motion County have not allowed the Motion Metropolitan Housing Authority to build any public housing for the poor or the elderly of the county within their boundaries." This statement tells who is doing what to whom, as well as when and where. Any group that wants action has to get definite. . . . Definiteness can empower a group.[19]

Part of being definite is to define the obvious. In the example above, what is "public housing"? What is the composition of the Metropolitan Housing Authority? Precisely what is its authority and how is it exercised? Have any organizations of the poor and elderly in the area expressed a demand for housing? When, and with what documentation? Fuzzy impressions begin to dissipate when you define the obvious. A clearer profile of the problem begins to emerge. This is not to say that accurate information is always easy to obtain. Often it is obscured by a cloud of public relations, or hidden behind a web of secrecy spun by those who have long-held influence. Thus, beware of your information source.

The most important reason for being specific is to identify probable targets for action. What agency, or official, or item of legislation appears to need our concentrated attention?

This underscores another strategic reality. Analytical thinking is never done neutrally. Each person or group doing the analysis of the problem has a point of view, a social location, a set of images about the situation, and some expectations for resolving the issue. In other words, ideology—one's social frame of mind—plays a role in defining any issue. When someone asserts that public housing is an improper function of government (though FHA-financed homes are O.K.), or if he opposes residential mixing of economic classes, then his ideology is showing. Ideological assumptions of quite a different sort are reflected in such a statement as, "Opponents of public housing are racist (which may be true for the most part, depending on the definition of "racist")."

Ideology is not something to be avoided so much as something to be understood and kept within bounds. Everyone has an ideology—a conceptual structure that undergirds social action either to realize change or to reinforce the *status quo*. Ideology becomes self-deceiving and collectively dangerous when a system of ideas is closed to new insight or given the status of ultimate (total) truth. On the positive side, one's ideology can be modified by new experiences, especially in a pluralistic society such as the United States today. Ideological pluralism makes modification of social viewpoints possible; it also makes exposure to differing viewpoints necessary.

In fact, it is a good habit of strategic thinking to seek out multiple sources of insight concerning any social problem or public-policy issue. As a general rule, the definition of any problem is only as good as the variety of knowledgeable sources consulted. These sources of insight are not necessarily written. Beyond the information available in documents, journals, books, and news media, the most crucial exposures come from personal contact with those who know the problem firsthand. These include:

a. Victims of the policy

Have the grievances, know how the policy impinges on people.

b. Leaders of action groups

Recognize handles, or can create ways to engage the issue.

c. Policy makers and administrators

Control or know the key decision points, define possible options.

d. Expert students of the problem

Have the analytical tools to explore the workings of the issue.

Out of this range of encounters, which will be ideologically mixed and factually rich, can come sharper awareness of the problem and ways to engage it. However, exposure may also induce a sense of confusion because the sources of information will probably disagree as to the origin of the problem and its solution. This brings us to a second element of strategic thinking.

2. Why does this problem (issue, policy) exist?

Or, How did it arise? The focus now shifts from problem identification to *explanation.* The question of why arises naturally out of a consideration of what is wrong. Obviously, to state the nature of a problem is also to begin to make judgments about its origin—to explain why. But too often we assume we know why, or enough about why, simply because we know what. The danger in this assumption is that our proposed solutions to problems will be ill-conceived, if not irrelevant.

To take a familiar example, Why do traffic deaths rise on holiday weekends? Predicting highway death tolls, as does the National Safety Council, may be useful information to makers of coffins, but all those tallies reported on radio and television fail to explain the toll. Is it due to some combination of the mass rush to reach a destination, or more driving after drinking, or unsafe vehicles and roads, or is it primarily a function of the increased number of cars on the road simultaneously (in which case the careful response is to leave the car in the garage, and the public task is to provide efficient mass transit)? Clearer explanation of causal factors would focus efforts to reduce highway fatalities.

A more significant example is to be found in the quest for a national population policy. After decades of official indifference, the country suddenly was awakened to the ecological crisis—environmental pollution, finite resources, too many people (probably three hundred million Americans by the end of the century). Suddenly, as in Paul Ehrlich's book *The Population Bomb,* the problem was perceived apocalyptically: people and pollution would produce massive ecocide in a couple of decades. Draconian measures were proposed: government licensing of parenthood, enforced sterilization, removal of all tax exemptions.

But after this phase of "scarifying" talk, more sober analyses of ecological issues revealed that the problem had a different profile: (*a*) Our toxic technology is the main cause of environmental deterioration (though population increase in developed countries is still devastating because of high per capita consumption of resources). (*b*) Population growth is already slowing down in developed countries while environmental deterioration continues to escalate. Most of the ecology action should, therefore, be directed not to a war on people, but to a war on ecological ignorance, resource waste, and major sources of pollution.

An even more striking example of the need for analytical thought is offered in the question: Why do urban "riots" and smaller acts of group violence happen? Conventional journalistic accounts and political rhetoric emphasize the contagion of "riffraff" or "outside agitator" theories. Collective violence is here seen as a breakdown of "law and order" due to criminal or irrational behavior. But serious research has underscored a different perspective. These theories emphasize absolute or relative deprivation aggravated by the unfulfilled promises of the power structure, or the breakdown of shared norms in times of mass migration, fragmentation of power elites, etc. It is also apparent that violence on the part of minorities is a reaction to oppression at the hands of a complacent society, a society oblivious to elementary demands for justice. The point of this review is that one's picture of "riot" causation makes a great deal of difference in responding to group violence. (Clue: avoid every simple explanation.)[20]

The illustrations above suggest the hazards of relying on conventional or superficial explanations of any issue before us. In fact it is a good rule of thumb to distrust the conventional or simple causal theories because they obscure crucial factors and few social problems have simple causes. Usually some very important, but rather hidden (latent), factors are being overlooked.

Tendencies to miss what is going on are further reinforced insofar as public officials and citizen groups worry
about symptoms and surface effects instead of root causes
of public crises. For example, recall the outcry over school
busing and the silence about long-range effects of segre-
gated education. Or consider the outrage over the killing
of policemen and prison guards in contrast to the public's
apathy about unequal administration of justice. And ponder all those years of indignant talk about waste in foreign
aid when few questions were raised about the military
juntas supported, or the dependency relationships created,
by U.S. military and economic assistance.

One question emerges rather insistently from these illustrations: How does a person or group keep from acting
out of misinformed emotion? The question exposes an
information dilemma, which runs as follows. Social action
groups can seldom wait for further research before making
judgments about the dynamic underlying a problem; but
action groups usually need to know more than they already do about the combination of forces impinging on a
specific policy question. This dilemma is not easily overcome, but knowing that everybody shares the dilemma
makes it more tolerable. The best advice to any group
may be to discover what they can over a short period
(usually a few weeks), and to think it through carefully
before jumping into the fray. Above all, seek the wisdom
of some of the people involved.

Certainly, serious actionists or action groups need to do
enough inquiring, reading, and thinking to arrive at careful, reasonable explanations of the problem or problems
being tackled. Furthermore, an action group should test
the results of its probes by "trying out" the explanation
informally on some knowledgeable consultants (the vari-

ety of consultants suggested earlier in this chapter). These contacts should extend beyond allies to include individuals who are neutral and even some who define the problem oppositely. Keep asking: Whom did we consult about what?

None of the above advice is offered with the promise of resolving complex issues. Complexity will remain, for the obvious reason that issues are shaped by an ever-changing combination of forces. Issues do not stand still for examination; they constantly take new forms. Neither issues nor policies are static; they are better viewed as temporary convergences of forces.

In fact, our understanding of any issue is conditioned by our perception of the forces operating in that particular circumstance. We never recognize all the forces, of course. But our thinking about what is going on can be disciplined through "force field analysis." As the late Kurt Lewin originally suggested, force field analysis anticipates that in relation to any issue there is a dynamic balance of forces working in roughly opposite directions. The forces with the initiative, pushing for change, are called driving forces; the defending forces, resisting the change, are called restraining forces. In contemplating the "odds" for and against successful implementation of any action plan, one must have as clear a picture as possible of the driving and restraining forces. Keep in mind that the restraining forces can have contrary action plans and may be quite capable of seizing the initiative. Thus it is important to do force field analysis not only from one's own point of view but also from the perspective of the major opponent group, and perhaps also from the viewpoint of third parties in the middle. Through force field analysis one can recognize strengths at the points of the opposition's weakness, while one tries not to give the opposition similar openings. (Force field analysis is also helpful in choosing an appropriate action goal and in gauging the merit of various tactics.)

The basic assumption behind force field analysis is that change takes place whenever an imbalance occurs between the sum of restraining forces and the sum of driving forces. The imbalance can occur due to altered magnitude of force, direction of force, or the addition of new types of force.[21] This kind of analysis is conflict oriented. It is a way of pinpointing the clashing group interests, objectives, and behaviors that impinge on any issue of public policy. When used with some care in a pluralistic setting, force field analysis highlights the fact that social policy initiatives develop out of temporary, even reluctant, compromises between groups with different interests and ideals.

The kind of analysis suggested here helps to clarify what is going on and why, simply because the analyst is forced to ask more questions to fill in the picture. For example, the word "force" figures prominently in the above paragraph. To what kind of force are we referring? If power is the capacity to produce an effect or to reduce opposition, then power (or force) should be appreciated for its variety. Raw force is not necessarily the power that moves. Cultural pressure for change can outstrip the administrative power of corporate entities. Ideas have power—e.g., self-determination, liberation, genuine community—and ideas lose power—e.g., defense of the "free world," technological progress, the Peace Corps. In other words, the analysis of any issue, and action to meet it, should take account of the varieties of power operating in the situation. Power can be:

Coercive	*Sapiential*
Military and police force	Knowledge and information
Utilitarian	*Persuasive*
Economic resources and administrative responsibility	Symbolic and normative pressure

Personal

Charismatic and skillful leaders

Each group involved in a public-policy struggle has a different combination of these power assets available to it. Much of the action is not at the level of exerting coercive force (which quickly becomes self-defeating). Of particular value to action groups is their own sapiential and persuasive power. They can make symbolic appeals and disseminate fresh information at points where holders of coercive and utilitarian power lack openness or credibility. But an action group will probably have little effect unless it also seeks influence with the wielders of economic and administrative power.

The most important step in determining just where a social-policy problem lies and what might be done about it is to analyze the utilitarian power that impinges on the situation. In order to get satisfactory action, it is essential to identify the governmental and economic structures that contribute, by their action or inaction, to the problem; and furthermore, to identify the key decision makers within those structures and the policies or practices they are fostering. Then one can specify needed changes.

Whenever such power-structure analysis is lacking, the action plan remains vague and unspecified. For it is axiomatic that to obtain reform from established institutions, the action group must assert (pinpoint, communicate, and if need be, publicize):

a. The factual basis for the grievance;
b. The specific legal provision or administrative rule involved; and
c. The precise remedy sought.

In other words, change agents need to document their grievances, to know the rules and limits of authority that obtain for each agency or official holding utilitarian power, and to propose remedies that can be achieved. This brings us to the formulation of action goals.

3. What should we do about the problem?

What is the action goal? What is our objective in response to this issue? Specifically, what are we trying to accomplish? In the process of setting and specifying goals, we move from "consciousness raising," issue exploration, the analysis of structures and powers, to action planning. Eventually, the question becomes: *Who will do what with whom by when?* While we keep clearly in mind where we want to go (the long-range ends that we value deeply), but recognize that there is no straight line from here to there, our social engagement requires patient organizational work—concentrating on issues that can be tackled, making coalitions and compromises, collecting the push power to change policies. In other words, we work away at concrete goals through practical activity in whatever institutional settings we find ourselves. Some operational guidelines for setting goals follow:

a. *Entertain goals that you want to, and can, do something about.* This is a counsel of realism about the interests of would-be change agents. The outcomes sought should be beneficial, not only to others, but to those who are investing themselves and their resources in the action. The goal must appeal to the actors as something *valuable and realizable* (both desirable and feasible). However, this is not to say that planning must proceed on a narrow base of self-interest, perceived only in bread-and-butter terms. It is possible to enlarge people's self-interest by referring to the common good that would result from a changed policy or structure. Even Saul Alinsky, known for his hard-nosed community organizing, urges change agents to appeal to the "wondrous quality of man that from time to time floods over the natural dams of survival and self-interest," all the while remembering the immediate community of interest that creates an organization.

"The organization is born out of the issues and the issues are born out of the organization," writes Alinsky. He also emphasizes the need to select targets that are vulnerable to the power of the would-be action group. "Organizations are built on issues that are specific, immediate, and realizable. . . . An issue is something you can do something about, but as long as you feel powerless and unable to do anything about it, all you have is a bad scene." [22] Don't stop with general grievances or settle for vague goals. The function of an effective action leader is to help the group move from bad scenes to urgent problems to specific issues to definite objectives.

b. *Determine the action goal together.* A solid action objective should be determined as a group decision and must fit the group's situation and resources. Goal-setting requires open dialogue, possibly with the abandonment of early choices and with the expectation that there will be some turnover in the group. One experienced action trainer, Robert Bonthius, observes that group decision is essential because practically everyone in the group has strings on him—namely, interests and responsibilities.

One group decided that the most effective short-range thing it could do about the lack of public housing in the county was to replace two of the five members of the housing authority board with two residents of public housing within the next three months (vacancies were upcoming). One member, a clergyman, said he'd have to drop out of the group. He explained that one of the two housing authority board members to be replaced was the chairman of the board of trustees of his church. Social action often fails because some members of the group cannot accept the goal. Reservations have to be surfaced and dealt with—even sought out.[23]

Real consent of the action group is necessary to arrive at a workable goal—a goal for which members of the group will actually work.

Even when a group is united in purpose and clear about its objective, it cannot reasonably expect to change a public policy or institutional practice working alone. Bonthius emphasizes, "There are necessary allies—organizations and their key people—you have to have with you if you are to continue work on your action goal." List the necessary allies and what kind of help is needed from each (approval, money, documentary evidence, legal advice, parallel action, influence with a body of "elites," etc.), and then do what is required to secure their support.

Consultation with probable allies should not wait until an action objective has been selected. Setting the goal *together* is a collaborative process. Articulation of a needed policy change is often complicated by the fact that different groups will have particular interests which lead them to emphasize different objectives. They may appear to share an awareness of a crisis situation, but they disagree sharply about what to do about it. Two or more action groups can only arrive at a shared objective by means of dialogue, negotiation, and by making some deals: "We will support you in this objective if you support us in that action. We have this power, you have that resource. Can we link up?" Thus are workable social action plans formulated.

c. *Seek structural outcomes.* Groups that are unclear about the focus of the social action process (see Chapters 2 and 3 are likely to be deflected into a preoccupation with personal- and cultural-change goals, or with community-service projects, unless the specific function of social action is kept before them. Those who emphasize personal-change goals usually come up with educational plans to develop positive attitudes toward needed reforms, to foster new insights, to disseminate information through learning groups and mass media. An educational approach has its place, probably as a supporting activity or secondary goal, but it should not be confused with making structural changes in institutions and policies. Arguments to the contrary—e.g., that we can't change the system by restructuring pieces of it, but only through personal life-style changes—need to be refuted explicitly. Those who want to start "a project that everyone can support" also threaten to deflect the group away from action and into a service effort.

Often, divergent approaches can be included as secondary or follow-up aspects of the basic strategy goal. Take for example the national (even international) lettuce boycott called by UFWOC in 1970 and again in 1972. It does rely on a life-style change by housewives and it provides for broad citizen education, but the main action is at the point of letting growers and supermarket management know, through organized group pressure, that the boycott is serious. Another example of combined approaches to a social need is evident in the quest for a fair metropolitan or countywide distribution of low-cost housing. A major housing strategy can combine several dimensions of involvement: from personal witness to community education, to the formation of low-cost housing corporations, to court tests, to pressure for changed legislative or administrative provisions, to facilitating a turnover of policy makers. Notice, however, as in the illustration under point b that a social action group should concentrate on changing the public policy or policy-making structure.

d. *Adjust the specific goal to fit the action opportunity.* The goal should be scaled to fit the capacities of the action group, and the goal should be in phase with real decision-making choices.

Questions of scale have to do primarily with the range of contacts—occupational, political, civic, educational—that members of the action group intend to make. Are they dealing with congressmen, the P.T.A., the police chief, a corporation vice-president, another community-action group, a university research team, an underground FM station, a TV station, the state human-relations commission, a regional convention? The focus and scale of action affect the choice of appropriate contacts and subject matter. These contacts must also be selected in the light of the capacities of the group. Do not necessarily assume that local contacts always take precedence over county, state, or national contacts. The scope of contacts can be extended, with assistance from established public affairs organizations.

The congressional vote, in 1971, to stop subsidizing development of the SST provides an excellent case in point of the importance of being in phase with real decision-making choices. *At that time* the issue of the SST provided the first real opportunity for an environmental coalition to act nationally. The SST, rather than auto-emission standards, opposition to nuclear facilities and tests, or efforts to stop the Alaska Oil Pipeline, etc., was *the* issue on which it was most opportune to concentrate in early 1971.

e. *Translate the action goal into operational steps.* When a particular goal is selected, it should be stated as concretely as possible. Where, when, and with whom will the change be sought? The objective can be specified in behavioral terms, with behavior focused on a prime target and on subtargets. For example, to achieve the goal of an adequate national program of income maintenance, the prime target would be Congress, and crucial subtargets would be legislative assistants, various members of Congress (those on pertinent committees, those from districts with much impacted poverty, and those who provide the swing vote), and leaders of organizations that are exerting, or could exert, influence on this issue. Linkages with other initiatives on this issue would also be quite important.

In specifying tasks, the action group should consider not only what it will do but also what it intends to persuade others to do. When we remember *action often combines push power from outside and influence from people inside,* it is necessary to think in terms of a cluster of activities all oriented to the one goal. Social ethicist Henry Clark offers a diagram somewhat like the one below as a conceptual tool for considering operational steps:

$$A_1 \xrightarrow[\;t_2\quad B\;]{\;t_1\quad A\;} X \left.\begin{array}{c} \\ \\ \\ \end{array}\right\} \to G \leftarrow Z \xleftarrow[\;F\quad t_6\;]{\;E\quad t_5\;} A_3$$

$$A_2 \xrightarrow[\;t_4\quad D\;]{\;t_3\quad C\;} Y$$

Agent$_1$ uses *tactics* t_1 and t_2 in carrying out program *activities* A and B to bring about event X (which is our *objective*) as our agreed-upon contribution to attaining *Goal* G (the attainment of which also requires the occurrence of events Y and Z, which are the subgoals being pursued through activities C, D, E, and F by Agents A_2 and A_3).[24]

This brings us to questions of tactics.

6

ANALYZING TACTICS

Let me suggest to you that we live on a vast plain on which there are a large number of castles. These castles, representing our institutions, are unguarded: the moats are empty and the drawbridges are down. All we have to do is walk into the castles—the old institutions—and take everything out of them that would be valuable for the future. It is necessary to tiptoe in because there are some people who will get mad if you disturb them. So you move quietly. Unfortunately, the people who have been trying to get change up to now haven't been satisfied to tiptoe in and take what they wanted. They have done it in a different way. They assembled outside the castle and they blew their trumpets and claimed they were coming in to take over. The defenders, in a last access of energy, felt challenged to try and defend the castle.[25]

Robert Theobald used the above analogy in a speech a few years ago to emphasize that change can be had, more often than not, without making a frontal assault on the existing setup. Or at least without announcing it. Threatening noise can be a useful tactic from a position of weakness (remember Gideon?), but why demand combat when there are more effective ways to proceed? Tactics are to be evaluated not for their style but for their workability as moves in a strategy to achieve a social goal. The strategic question is (continuing the line of questions from Chapter 5):

4. How shall we move to attain the objective?

Where are the action handles? Everywhere. In this discussion, the word "tactics" refers to forms of action chosen and used by social action groups to reach a desired goal. Tactical moves are the array of activities and techniques initiated to get a target person and institution to change policy or structure in the direction of justice. These methods of action must be appropriate to the participants' situation and objective. The next few pages can only begin to unpack the meaning of the three sentences above.

a. *Tactics are consciously chosen from an array of possible activities and techniques.* Tactics can include: awareness-building, citizens lobbying, electoral politics, petitioning, lawsuits, corporate proxy challenges, selective patronage, picketing, demonstrative acts, rallies, and such "hard-nosed" behavior as harassment, perturbation of systems, strikes, mass presences, and civil disobedience. To cite a current source of information, each of these tactical options is reviewed in *Earth Tool Kit: A Field Manual for Environmental Action* (Pocket Books, 1971), Section II. (To think that all these tactics might be used for ecological objectives is rather startling to persons who think of environment as a "motherhood" issue. Achieving a quality environment *is* a conflict-laden process.)

The listing of these tactical possibilities ought to remind us that any number can play the social action game. Learning how is a matter of some watching, a little coaching, and much copying (resulting in a high percentage of fumbles, interceptions, and "smears" for the unwary). Interestingly enough, *people with differing, even contradictory, goals tend to have similar choices when it comes to action tactics.* Although there are many different groups of players and styles of play, there is a fascinating tendency among them to match one another's techniques. Mass communications, especially, have given wide currency to action tactics (some useful, some merely fashionable). This has happened to such a degree that the tactics can become relatively autonomous from the ends they serve. In other words, people undertaking social action have in common not so much particular policy goals as a set of available action tactics. *But what they are least likely to agree on are the appropriate tactics for any particular situation and objective.* Groups can fall apart over questions of tactics.

Rather than discussing a list of tactics here, I shall put them in strategic perspective. Our choice of tactics at any given time should be disciplined by the ways we think the goal can best be reached. Four ways, or basic approaches, have been suggested in an unpublished paper by George Younger of the Metropolitan Urban Service Training Facility.[26] These four approaches to social change are:

—Cooperation

If you control the terms of participation and keep your eye on the activity of the insiders, cooperation is a viable way to gain influence over a system. But if the existing order is allowed to set the terms with minimal negotiation, then the system merely co-opts the cooperator. (Toby Moffett, *The Participation Put-On: Reflections of a Disenchanted Washington Youth Expert* [Delta Books, 1971], offers an instructive report on the hazards of cooptation by government agencies.) The task is to sell your objectives or programs to those already having responsibility, monitoring the implementation, and helping them to evaluate the results. It can be a matter of "helping" them to live up to existing rules, or of picking up an area of policy-planning and implementation. Younger offers the example of an urban renewal plan. The neighborhood organization cooperates with the overall design principles and fills in the local details.

—Replacement
It does make a difference who runs the system and any important subsystems. These persons are either elected, appointed, or work themselves into that position. Although to the casual observer they may not appear vulnerable, a threat to replace them can open the door to cooperation. For example: "We have a congressman in our section of town who has been challenged in the primary every two years. As a result, his own statements of policy and those of the groups he relates to have become more and more like his opposition's sentiments." Younger warns that a threat to replace the people in control of an aspect of policy must be backed up by a willingness to step in because when confronted they just might say: "All right. Who will come over and help us change it?"

—Opposition
This means keeping the heat on to make "them" change policy. Most groups that are self-defined "activists" take this approach. Working from outside, they want to stay there, which poses a problem if some of their objectives begin to be achieved, or if the authorities neutralize that kind of protest. Saul Alinsky tells about the head of a corporation who showed him blueprints for a large ground-

floor area of a new plant. "See that big hall? That's our sit-in room! When the sit-inners come they'll be shown in and there will be coffee, TV, and good toilet facilities—they can sit here until hell freezes over." However, this problem will not arise most of the time, since the Establishment gives ground grudgingly and prefers the appearance of responsiveness to the granting of real concessions.

—Parallel system

The object is to create services and structures that government or business will not provide, and to move toward the formation of *counter-institutions*. Some obvious examples are: gypsy cab companies, tenants' rent strike funds, freedom schools, self-developed community security corps, even transnational peace groups. "Let us handle it ourselves," is the rallying cry of parallel systems. If the service activity or organizing structure becomes an auxiliary of the regular system, then it ceases to be parallel and becomes cooperative, or even co-opted. A striking current example of parallel system is to be found in some OEO-funded legal-service programs for the poor. The hostility of other governmental agencies and officials toward these legal-service cadres suggests they are genuinely parallel. Citizens lobbies, such as Common Cause and the Coalition on National Priorities are also counter-institutional structures.

This brief overview of four approaches to tactics should not be construed as requiring a hard-and-fast choice. It is a matter of recognizing what you are doing at any given time, keeping in mind alternate approaches. Concludes Younger: "You may try cooperation for a while and find you have to be in opposition. Or you may try working inside the system and find you cannot get what you are after that way, so you go outside the system. . . . [In any case] there is no substitute for organized methods of getting together the groups of people that you have access to, and worrying about how they relate to and work with other groups."

b. *Tactics are flexible, in order to have institutional impact.* They are chosen in the free flow of action and reaction. As discussed in Chapter 4, the realistic radical is open to a creative mix of tactics. Using "tactics" means using the resources you have to do what you can. Effectiveness requires not fashionable, but fitting behavior, sometimes accenting *protest* and at other times stressing *reform.* Appropriate tactics cannot be classified as either militant or moderate. The point is illustrated by Charles V. Hamilton, coauthor of *Black Power,* who rejected "the meaningless game" of trying to out-relevant or out-militant the opposition.

In the final analysis it will be the substance of organization, not the symbols, that will advance the race. It will be the reality of group cohesion, not the rhetoric of mind blowing, that will contribute to survival. It will be the actual talent of acquired knowledge and skills, not the mere talk of being relevant, that will lead to our economic and political development. The sooner we can get away from the simplistic dichotomies of "reformist" vs. "revolutionary," "moderate" vs. "militant," etc., the sooner we can get on with the business of taking care of business.[27]

Since that observation was made in 1969, minority communities seem to have set aside stylistic arguments in order to concentrate on "getting to" the policy makers and the resources they control. Even the Black Panther party, once the epitome of "dangerous" militance in the eyes of whites, is changing. "We cannot jump from A to Z as some thought," said Huey Newton recently. "Our intention to operate with reality does not mean we accept things the way they are. We'll operate within the system so we can change it."

But the white majority is still preoccupied with questions of rhetorical style, e.g., warmly endorsing the black capitalism of Leon Sullivan but automatically condemning the black communism of Angela Davis.

Predominantly white churches still tend to mirror the majority's knee-jerk reaction to confrontational tactics on the part of insistent nonwhites. Thus the major denominations were "shocked" by James Forman's visitations in 1969, and disputed for months, not the programmatic goals of the Black Manifesto, but the fact that Forman *demanded* reparations after issuing a *revolutionary*-sounding preamble. It was argued, then, that Forman's tactics were counterproductive because they produced such vocal initial reaction. But in retrospect, we can see that temporarily heated conflict in the church was a sign of real institutional confrontation. Subsequently, several denominations established funds for the self-development of economically and politically deprived people, in an effort to respond to the *growing* gap between rich and poor at home and overseas. Furthermore, some of those who detested the demands and resisted the new directions most vociferously began to make substantial common cause with "moderate" groups such as the Urban League, the NAACP, and the OIC—groups they did not visibly support in the '60s.

Basic dynamics of institutional change in response to confrontation tactics have been well summarized by social ethicist Max Stackhouse:

The character of most institutions in our society is such that dramatic and immediate change upon demand is not likely. The institutions are both stable enough and open enough that protest can be made. But the protest is only partially heard and seldom taken seriously in the terms proposed. Such reception of protest is neither merely "co-optation" nor "repressive toleration" as believed by the new sectarians of today's left. It is much more subtle than that. Exterior protest and demand can serve as catalytic forces, but in the absence of collapse or cataclysm, interior change occurs through incremental steps.

In short, there is a dialectical relationship between exterior pressures and interior restructuring of priorities. The exterior "radicals" do not get what they want, and despair even more of institutions that they did not like anyway. By their statement of "what is necessary," however, radicals establish a counter-balance to the overwhelming voice of "moderates" who dominate any institution. Moderates always accent "what has been done." The progressives are freed thereby to explore "what is possible," although they are alternately cursed and claimed by both radicals and moderates.[28]

Confrontation tactics become dubious, not because they are used, but when they become gestures without constructive follow-up. Confrontation can publicize need and can even shock institutions out of inertia, but it does not in itself produce programs. A collaborative approach, practicing the art of the possible as well as the art of protest, is likely to be most effective.

c. *Creative tactics maintain or construct opportunities for institutional response.* Institutions under pressure or undergoing shock need to be helped toward constructive response. This requires the cooperation of others besides those administering the shock or registering the grievance. One of the necessary steps in institutional change is to gain support or reinforcement from some of the holders of corporate power. This is more likely to happen if their immediate survival is not threatened.

Thus, corporate insiders who may be ready to shift priorities and change policies should not be forced by the outsiders to declare themselves for or against the policy under attack, but should be encouraged to participate in the new thrust, and be shown the benefits of doing so. Also they need time to adjust and may welcome specific input that can be formulated into new policies. Attention should be focused on the desired change by means of both informal suggestion (or dialogue) and formal recommendation. Bureaucracies, executive planners, and administrators abhor a vacuum. It is often a matter of knowing the right time to make a better recommendation and the combination of initiatives that are likely to get it accepted. The idea, after all, is to zero in on *targets*—"the persons and institutions who must be persuaded, forced, manipulated, beguiled or in some way moved to enact, allow, or cooperate with change." [29]

On the other hand, institutional decision makers are seldom activated one by one, because they are "captive" to a limited ethos and structure. That pattern is more likely to be broken when they are organized or at least have a sense of group identity. Happily, there is a growing corporate underground, staffed by "Naderized" rebels in double-knit suits. It also operates in government, as evidenced by leaks of secret minutes of crucial meetings, such as the "Anderson papers." There are even underground corporate newspapers designed to counteract unethical and initiative-killing company practices. The movement is restless, creative, and uninterested in personal publicity.

This illustration points to an emerging dimension of

social action—namely, the desire to construct supportive mechanisms (made up of kindred spirits and like-minded colleagues) for people in corporate enterprises who are desirous of being change agents. Furthermore, if social action is to be institutionally effective, it is essential to develop and maintain linkages among networks of consultants, legitimators in the corporate hierarchy, and groups putting on action pressure from outside.

d. *Available tactics are shaped by the situation(s) of the participants.* "Situation" refers to social or organizational setting, previous experience, a stake in the outcome. Perhaps no one has been more influential in stimulating a situational approach to tactics than Saul Alinsky. He makes no bones about the fact that groups use tactics according to their resources and interests. His illustrations come out of decades of mass-based community organization among the urban "Have-Nots" (mastering the politics of scarcity).

For an elementary illustration of tactics, take parts of your face as the point of reference: your eyes, your ears, and your nose. First, the eyes: if you have organized a vast, mass-based people's organization, you can parade it visibly before the enemy and openly show your power. Second, the ears: if your organization is small in numbers, then do what Gideon did: conceal the members in the dark but raise a din and clamor that will make the listener believe that your organization numbers many more than it does. Third, the nose: if your organization is too tiny even for noise, stink up the place.

Always remember the first rule of power tactics: Power is not only what you have but what the enemy thinks you have. Power has always derived from two main sources, money and people. Lacking money, the Have-Nots must build power from their own flesh and blood.[30]

They can use the vote, organize neighborhoods, selectively boycott or harass companies, visit city hall, set up parallel structures—all the while enjoying themselves, to the alarm of the power structure. Against the finesse and sophistication of the *status quo,* they must be blunt and abrasive. (After picking the institutional target, "freeze it, personalize it, and polarize it.") But they can also cause the enemy's own undoing through such techniques as ridicule or by making the holders of power try to live up to their own book of rules. ("The real action is the enemy's reaction.")

Alinsky, despite his flair for the dramatic, does not advocate self-indulgent protest. In fact, he implies that protest is always a two-edged sword. Protest can be turned back on the action group by a wily target institution that organizes public support in defense of present policy. Therefore, it is essential for protestors to organize Establishment support. (For example, Rochester's community organization called FIGHT organized "Friends of FIGHT," among suburbanites.)

If Alinsky-style conflict tactics are effective in urban centers, to what extent are they transferable to middle-class communities and action groups? Is it possible to "liberate" middle America the same way? Not exactly, though Alinsky's general wisdom applies, and some of the newer methods of action he helped devise are actually tailored for the nonpoor. One of these is the "proxy tactic," in which certain shareholders appear at stockholders' meetings to vote their shares against selected company recommendations, or assign their votes as shareholders to a group organized to push for change in corporation policies. Also it should be remembered that there is an increasing number of both "new poor" and "powerless" people in outer cities and suburbs who feel victimized by institutional forces. The situation of these "unyoung, unpoor, unblack" middle Americans, although hardly as depressed as that of the poor, is not all that different. They also lack power to control their lives, the quality of which is eroding. But they have "been had" by the Establishment in that their alienation has been channeled downward against the poor and the black, or sideward against the young. Now, perhaps, they are ready to direct their anger at the managers of the power structure and to work for social policies that liberate people from a dehumanizing technology, and that affirm pluralism rather than pitting community groups against one another.

How will middle America work for this kind of change? By means that fit the suburbs and that relate them to metropolitan problems. One such model is described by Gabriel Fackre, who participated in the formation of a successful independent newsweekly in a medium-sized Pennsylvania city. By providing responsible news coverage through LIP (*Lancaster Independent Press*), a citizens group used information as a social action tool. They covered subjects of youth culture, housing difficulties, the workings of local government, peace action, etc., in the late 1960's. The above example illustrates what it takes to get social movement at the community level. Beginning with a dedicated core (a self-trained team of reporters, editors, composers, distributors), involving a broad base (a constituency of subscribers), the citizens group maintained a situational focus (subject matter of LIP met the needs of readers) and acquired Establishment allies (endorsements from community accreditors, people with special resources).[31]

The newspaper approach to social change is reflective

of the tendency of middle-class and suburban people to play the action game in a less confrontational, though not always less dramatic, way. They proceed according to their occupational talents, acquired social manners, and preference for orderly procedure. However, this does not exclude a willingness to join in demonstrative acts, such as fasting, prayer vigils, or even street theater in order to advocate policy changes. Any of these tactics can communicate effectively if they are done by people who look "straight" and if they receive some coverage in the media. One group which was using such tactics made itself available for radio talk shows which followed up the events, thus communicating much more extensively than through the act itself. Again, this illustrates the importance of a mix of tactics to fit the preferences of participants.

One important way to bridge participants' situations is to *plan for various degrees of involvement.* Especially where the action goal encompasses several objectives and a range of tactical efforts, it is helpful to take a cue from Hans Spiegel, who suggested ten years ago that strategic intervention into the social system can include first party, second party, third party, and fourth party action. Here it can be illustrated in terms of efforts to eliminate an unfair military draft.

First party interveners openly challenge existing policy and move to reconstruct it. This might entail, or has entailed, group draft resistance, underground transport for draft exiles and deserters, harassment of local boards, organizing a draft repeal campaign, or working for amnesty without strings.

Intervention as a *second* party occurs through support groups providing such assistance as identifying personally with a particular protest, becoming a cosponsor, providing legal aid to resisters and conscientious objectors who were denied claims, ministering to draft exiles, bringing a veterans group into the draft-repeal effort, or exposing the hidden inequities in the lottery.

Intervention as a *third* party involves mediation between opposing parties, such as efforts to obtain clarification of Selective Service rulings or a review of a specific case (the lottery doesn't eliminate unfair regulations), or to provide a community education program on draft problems.

Intervention as a *fourth* party entails only indirect support by means of resolutions, objective counseling services, or financial support of first, second, or third party efforts. A wise social action leader plans for these varying degrees of involvement, so as to avoid unnecessary division over tactics, or fragmentation due to several objectives.

e. *Appropriate tactics fit the strategic goal.* It might appear to the casual reader of the methods outlined above that almost any tactics are judged permissible if they work (so long as you don't try to work them against me). Well, let's see. Is it better to be open about the ends-means relationship, or is it better to be obsessed with the ethics of means? On a straight utilitarian basis

the man of action . . . asks of ends only whether they are achievable and worth the cost; of means, only whether they will work. . . . The means-and-end moralists or non-doers always wind up on their ends with any means. . . . The ethics of means and ends varies inversely with one's personal interest in the issue. . . . The less important the end to be desired, the more one can afford to engage in ethical evaluations of means. . . . Success or failure is a mighty determinant of ethics. . . . Any effective means is automatically judged by the opposition as being unethical.[32]

Quite a sardonic statement. Single-mindedly it asserts the need to judge both tactics and goals in context according to their consequences (extrinsically). In other words, does this particular goal justify these particular action methods? The question can be redefined to read: Which tactics will work most directly for what gains at whose loss? One can even phrase it with reference to a Biblical teaching; namely, judge the tactics by the fruits they produce institutionally.

But consequences are notoriously hard to gauge in advance. Sometimes the side effects are worse than the gain being sought. And people are always kidding themselves about the benign consequences of their actions. Tactics only make sense as part of a strategy. They have to "fit" into the whole picture. The fitting response arises out of a more holistic view of what is responsible, not merely of what works. The utilitarian calculus needs to be enriched by understandings of what is right and wrong (intrinsically). In this perspective one works under moral obligation and proceeds by methods that he would want universalized.

For example, principles of liberty, justice, and general welfare have an intrinsic, or nonnegotiable value. On those obligatory grounds, human dignity is not to be violated. The cynic who points out that human dignity is violated all the time misses the point. It is still very wrong to offend or eliminate the human rights of others, even when it may seem to help our cause.

For reasons of both pragmatism and principle, social action tactics generally exclude violent action. By violent action is meant, not a little disruption, but hard-core resistance techniques such as insurgency, kidnapping, assassination, sabotage, armed propaganda, the *coup d'état*. Along with some forms of the strike, these classic tactics of direct action (over against social and political action) are aimed not at changing institutions but at intimidating or eliminating opponents.[33] Readers of this chapter are unlikely to find themselves in extreme situations that justify anything terroristic. The fact that self-styled saboteurs and security agents provocateur are active does not make them legitimate; it simply underscores the need for more open and responsive democratic process. Only in states or areas of society where voluntary association for sociopolitical purpose is forbidden or violently repressed are social movements bound to become conspiratorial and to employ violent counteraction. Here we are not discussing what form responsible action should take where an unjust government tyrannizes the people.

It makes no moral sense to romanticize collective violence as a "cure" for cultural crisis as did the French romantic Georges Sorel. His influential book *Réflexions sur la Violence* (1908) proposed that social reform, democracy, and humanism made people soft and that proletarian violence would help them recover the old energy and élan. His rejection of compromise and his glorification of violent action foreshadowed Fascism. The myth of proletarian violence, of course, is not nearly so influential on the American scene as is the "shoot-out theory" of dealing with lawbreakers. This legend of the Old West assumes that the "good guys" can put away the "bad guys" by means of violence. (As Carl Ogelsby quipped: "Fifteen minutes of violence, then nice things.")

But violent action from any source, whether initiated by citizens or government, begets more violence. Violence reflects futility, a loss of political imagination. In most situations there is an alternative—to act by means of nonviolent pressure. (I join Robert McAfee Brown as a "selective conscientious objector" to violence.) [34] Nonviolent tactics by citizens groups can include creative disobedience, noncooperation, confrontation, resistant behavior. Each of these approaches seeks to overcome unjust policy while respecting the just exercise of civil authority.

Civil disobedience fits in at this point. No amount of official rhetoric to the contrary can erase the fact that, even in a democracy, groups of people will defy policies they consider dumb, unfair, or evil. This can happen under certain political conditions suggested by Hannah Arendt:

> Civil disobedience arises when a significant number of citizens have become convinced either that the normal channels of change no longer function, and grievances will not be heard or acted upon—as in the case of the striking mailmen—or that, on the contrary, the government is about to change, and has embarked upon or persists in modes of action whose legality and Constitutionality are open to grave doubt [such as waging the Vietnam war without a clear congressional declaration]. . . . In other words, civil disobedience can be tuned to necessary and desirable change or to necessary and desirable preservation or restoration of the status quo. . . . In neither case can civil disobedience be equated with criminal disobedience.[35]

If justice is an ideal balance of competing interests which the law ought to promote, then strict enforcement of existing law may be unjust. Sometimes the wiser course is to bend or change the law rather than to punish the disobedient. When disobedient individuals or groups are threatened with, or subjected to, harsh penalties by government, the result is both to "chill" open dissent and to "fuel" underground resistance. The confrontation of the Federal Government with the "Harrisburg 7" (Philip Berrigan and six others) is a painful reminder of the age-old conflict between the requirements of law and the dictates of conscience.

There is no escape from the task of judging every action, whether of obedience or of disobedience to law, by a full-orbed moral scrutiny. The claim of law is a valid ingredient in this matrix but not an overriding one. To except any particular kind of behavior from moral criticism because it enjoys the status of a legal obligation is to settle for a view of the state's authority at odds with everything for which our political heritage stands.[36]

Space does not permit further exploration of this complex subject. Suffice it to conclude that our tactics should be congruent with our goals. *Sound tactics serve concrete social goals by increasing the base of active support, neutralizing the power of the opposition, and moving those who control institutional structures to act constructively.* Since social action concentrates on altering systems that violate human well-being, some of the tactics will have to be *militantly nonviolent.*

5. *What are the action results?*

How has the action altered the situation? The "situation" is both the *goal* being sought and the *group* doing the acting. What is happening to us and to our group? Evaluation, to have validity, should be done by at least several members of the action organization, rather than by isolated individuals. Insight needs to be pooled concerning:

> the goal outcome—to what degree achieved?
> the target group—how influenced or changed?
> related or adjacent structures—how affected?
> popular value systems—how altered?
> process and goals—how congruent?

fate of our action system—developing or terminating?

This process of evaluation is not to be confused with periodic invitations for feedback or expressions of "feeling" about the group. Strategic evaluation is something more objective, externally focused, concentrated on discerning outcomes.

Evaluation is a continuous process because the situation is fluid, and decisions usually have to be made cumulatively. (One does not work out all the details and then decide to act on a social issue.) From this point of view, evaluation is quite similar to decision-making—only the verb tenses change. The decision maker asks: Is it . . . ? or, Will it . . . ? The evaluator asks: Was it . . . ? or, Did it . . . ? Evaluation is perhaps most precise when it is carried out as a review of a decision already made. Consider this approach. *On strategic occasions, when deciding what to do:*

a. List all relevant alternatives that come to mind.
b. Reject those that reveal a crippling objection.
   (1) require means that are not available (Is it feasible?)
   (2) violate our basic values (Is it ethical?)
   (3) alienate necessary supporters (Will it stick?)
c. Evaluate the feasibility, ethics, and probable degree of support for those alternatives not rejected.
d. Choose one alternative, if necessary by random choice (otherwise known as drawing straws).

Before implementing:

a. Fragment into sequential steps.

   Serial action is good politics (and easier to evaluate).

   A strategic reserve is useful (so save some assets).

   Postpone the more costly choices, if possible.

   b. Consider new information (or arrange for it).

Evaluate while implementing: review the above steps.[37]

   a. Make time for this review.

   b. Write it out briefly.

Laugh a little.

Finally, *never settle for winning*. Many a social policy has been emasculated after legislative enactment or executive announcement. *On occasion retreat*. Chances are the target institutions and policy makers will provide a new opportunity. *Be alert for unanticipated consequences*. Especially expect to be "frustrated" by the outcome of any particular policy battle. Often the holders of power will respond to a grievance in terms that are less than satisfactory—you get "half a loaf." Both the concept and structure of a policy change can be quite different than expected, since other forces are acting in the situation as well. In this sense, social problems are never "solved," but more or less constructive steps can be taken to deal with them.

7

AND THE CHURCH?

How does the church fit into the social action process discussed in the preceding chapters? This question deserves brief treatment here, not only because the author is professionally involved but also because the church is a major voluntary association with a pivotal social role. The church both influences and is influenced by the larger society's moral ferment. As Richard Cornuelle noted in the mid-'60s, churches are part of the "independent" sector, able to move in and out of both "public" and "private" sectors. At their best, the religious communities make considerable contact with urgent personal and public needs.

The social capability of the churches increases to the extent that they take a comprehensive moral view of public affairs and to the degree that they relate to a diversity of social groups. Churches can transcend the specialization that fragments the big moral issues, and they can learn about social reality from their own internal conflicts. Most regional and national church bodies have actually experienced confrontations across lines of race, class, and age; stirrings of radical left and radical right; early expressions of the civil rights, peace, and women's equality movements; and the thrust of self-determination among deprived people at home and overseas. Unfortunately, many church members do not yet appreciate these social encounters, nor do they grasp the potentiality of the church to act in society.

The major power assets available to churches for purposes of social action are: a transforming *message,* extensive *membership,* and considerable *money.* Here we will consider these power assets in reverse order of importance. Remember that we are talking about *potential* power, which often fails to materialize. One finds in many church settings that these assets are obscured by, or "tied up in," routine religion, rather than being put to work for social change. The assets only make a social action difference when the message is clearly translated, the members coherently organized, and the money specifically applied.

Church Money Power

The churches and synagogues of America control roughly $80 billion worth of real estate, and $20 billion invested in securities. Furthermore, $7 billion a year are contributed by the members. When viewed as a whole, this is considerable wealth. But control of these assets is in the hands of many separate and diffuse ecclesiastical structures. Notice also that we are contemplating the gross cumulative holdings of the three major faith groups—Protestants, Catholics, and Jews.

Organized religion is one of the most differentiated, if not fragmented, institutions in modern society. It has many denominational structures—among Protestants alone, a score of separately organized large denominations and over two hundred smaller ones—each servicing a network of local congregations. Each congregation in turn has its own capital assets and operating budget, and depends on offerings to make ends meet. Thus we see that church wealth is quite decentralized.

Much of the real estate consists of local church buildings and grounds; much of this property is heavily mortgaged or requires costly maintenance. However valuable this property may be, relatively little of it is likely to be converted into liquid assets. Still, some congregations are in a position to transfer valuable property (or income from property) to community groups for their use and development.

What about the investment portfolios of the churches? Again, control of investments is decentralized, with small sums in local church endowment funds and the rest scattered among denominational agencies. Nevertheless, the major denominations have accumulated considerable investment portfolios in order to pay clergy pensions and to support specialized staff and programs.

Until the late '60s, the investment responsibility of churches was viewed almost entirely in terms of adequate return for the dollars invested. Few questions were asked about the employment practices and production decisions of corporations in which churches hold stock. But church bodies began to insist on nondiscriminatory employment practices on the part of contractors, suppliers, hotels, etc., with which the churches do business. Similarly church groups began to raise questions about the responsibility of corporations, not only toward racially excluded Americans, but also toward oppressed people overseas (e.g., in southern Africa).

Gradually, under the pressure of publicity about their holdings,[38] investment committees of the churches began to scrutinize *both* employment practices *and* production decisions of corporations in which the churches own stock.

In order to challenge the perpetuation of racism, the manufacture of military weapons, or the policies of environmental destruction, segments of the church have initiated or joined in petitions of management and various proxy proposals—e.g., to expose Gulf Oil Corporation's operations in Angola, to halt the manufacture and sale of napalm by Dow Chemical Corporation, to communicate with Honeywell, Inc., about its production of antipersonnel mines, and, beginning with Campaign GM, to urge corporations to invest in serious antipollution efforts. On the whole, church agencies have tried to use their stock as leverage on corporations, rather than seeking purity for the church by means of immediate divestment (because the latter tactic leaves the corporate practice unchanged).[39]

An investment strategy designed to challenge socially injurious economic practices does not, in itself, transfer church-owned resources directly to the powerless. The transfer of resources occurs at present through: (1) grants made possible by investment earnings, (2) investment in high-risk, low-return development enterprises, and (3) creation of special funds for community self-development. Through the use of special offerings, this third approach is now occurring on a larger scale than the other two. By means of self-development funds, denominations such as The United Presbyterian Church U.S.A. and The United Methodist Church are responding to the thrust of self-determination—affirming the right of people to have dignity, self-respect, and a real voice in deciding how their needs shall be met. The object is to stop being paternalistic and to start being more of an advocate for the powerless.

In place of voluntary paternalism, which for so long characterized the social service efforts of churches, as well as of civic groups and community agencies, the new emphasis is on disciplined *corporate voluntarism,* whereby social programs are determined cooperatively and planned carefully with clients.[40] A valid (i.e., nonpaternalistic) social program must seek to effect real changes for the benefit of a presently deprived and disadvantaged community and to involve that community in the process of effecting those changes. The program should be aimed at long-term correction of conditions and not merely at providing short-term emergency assistance. These principles of self-development, now accepted in church planning, have implications for government and business as well. By granting funds according to needs defined with clients, the churches help to set the institutional pace. Of course, some of the results, especially where the funds go for community *action,* are unsettling to church members who are still thinking in traditional terms.

The Potential of Church Members

The many millions of church members (who are for the most part democratically organized and well educated) constitute a potent asset when they are "turned on" to issues of public affairs. But relatively few church members imagine themselves acting for justice through the church. As yet, they are not thinking in corporate terms about using church money and manpower in strategic ways to make a social difference. Instead, many adherents merely expect the church to provide a sanctuary of inspiration and warmth in a confusing, impersonal world, and to leave all matters of social involvement to individual discretion.

As shown in a recent North American Interchurch Study,[41] most church members in the United States see the mission of the church as "oriented to individuals." They rank as important functions: winning others to Christ; providing worship for members; providing religious instruction, ministerial services, and sacraments; and helping the needy. Pastors in the United States generally agree, except that they also "perceive the church serving as social conscience to the community," ranking this ahead of sacraments. Among functions not considered important for the local church are: "supporting minority groups, building low-cost housing, influencing legislation, and providing fellowship activities for members." It would appear from this survey that church people are disinterested in social action from a church base and will resist church efforts in this direction. But the research indicates that the main reason for member withdrawal is *not* "social involvement," but an unchallenging experience of church life. The survey reveals that apathy, not anger, is the dominant factor in the decline of church member support.

It would seem wiser for churchmen to design creative social action opportunities than for them to avoid social action so as to keep congregations "happy." Certainly there is enough talent among the membership to make such ventures possible. But the interest and talent must be mobilized.

Clergymen share responsibility with laymen for providing, or failing to provide, social action leadership. Even in their roles as social educators, not to mention action planners, clergymen more often than not duck social issues. For example, relatively few sermons contain substantial public-issue content. *Psychology Today* (April, 1970) carried a report on a survey of Protestant ministers from nine major denominations in California. Researchers Foster, Glock, Quinley, and Stark found that in the late '60s, there was much silence on all the prominent public issues, such as the black-white confrontation, the grape strike, and the Vietnam war. Only 25 percent of the pastors surveyed had given at least five sermons during 1968 that dealt mainly with controversial questions. Only 54 percent said they frequently discussed public affairs with members of their congregation in the course of their pastoral duties. They justified their silence on the grounds that it was not their role and that it would disturb the equilibrium of the congregation.

But *not* all congregations and members are undergoing pacification. Here and there one finds the influence of younger clergy of all races and of a significant percentage of laymen "who are no longer content to see the church remain an institution where the socially and economically advantaged can seek comfort and reassurance that their view of the world is really right." [42] They support church participation in social action and expect it to occur through a more disciplined, informed, and self-giving membership.

The socially activist members are proceeding in a variety of styles (see the Appendix), often through task groups of members and sometimes through special missionary-structured (or issue-oriented) congregations. These special congregations tend to remain small and ecumenical since they are consciously organized to be communities of social change. One such congregation with membership drawn from established congregations in a middle-sized city describes itself as

a community of Christians committed to a specific mission —community service and social action. We hope to build a finer environment by corporate action with others who care. Our goal is community change through reconciliation. All members are involved in mission. We will focus attention on our specific mission, knowing that other Christians are working in other areas of the church's ministry.

The last sentence of this statement clearly indicates that such a ministry is an exception to the prevailing pattern of local church life. As a novel alternative of modest proportions, the issue-oriented congregation is a parallel church institution, which also functions as a cooperative auxiliary structure. The people who join it are ready to act. Thus, the three-year-old Congregation for Reconciliation in Dayton, Ohio, reported a confrontation with the National Cash Register Co. over questions of equal opportunity, a United People campaign plan to challenge United Fund priorities, and exploration of Gulf Oil's corporate responsibility in Angola.[43]

That kind of activity (i.e., first party intervention) is unusual at the local church level. Frequently, it is backed up by second party action on the part of more traditionally organized congregations, or regional and national church bodies, as these bodies issue social policy statements and implement follow-up programs of education and action.

Of course, social action oriented church groups and their ecclesiastical supporters are criticized by some church members in the more traditional parishes who see no reason why groups of pastors and laymen should spend significant energy outside the flock except for purposes of gaining new members. Members of the more traditional parish churches usually expect the church to avoid social intervention beyond the level of third or fourth party (see Chapter 6). Their objections are typically couched in procedural terms—e.g., "The church should not take corporate action on social issues"—though what they resist most strongly is any initiative by church groups to change social structures. Sociologists of religion are finding that conservative laymen and clergy make a sharper distinction between individual service and structural change than they do between action undertaken by individuals and corporate action by church bodies.[44] The conservative wing of the church wants *not* to challenge the social *status quo,* but to rescue individual souls.

Church historian Martin Marty observes toward the close of his recent book *Righteous Empire: The Protestant Experience in America,* that well-heeled representatives of the "approved world" prefer to support religious approaches that are pessimistic about achieving real social reform and are content to rescue the individual who is then invited, if he will, to save others. Churches or church groups with this orientation may not actually ignore all public needs, but their social involvement is quite likely to stop at the point of providing some volunteer casework to aid casualties of the system, or at the point of supporting community programs that have an individual service orientation. This kind of religion poses little threat to those who hold political power because it does not raise questions of collective morality or structural reform. Rather, it tends to vent restless emotions while it provides warmth for troubled souls.

Over against this tradition of the *rescuers,* as Marty calls them, is another tradition that evolved from the Calvinist movement. It is the tradition of the *transformers,* who read in the Bible a message of human solidarity and a promise of world transformation. This message translates into an expectation of social reform in which struggle the church should actively participate. Rather than agreeing simply to heal individual hurts, the transformation-minded church is also interested in helping to renew and even redraft the social contract.

Finding Direction in the Message

The greatest power asset of the church in society is not money or members as such, but the message which the church bears. The money alone makes the church just another cautious institution. The members as such are a very diverse crowd of people. But the message makes of this conglomeration a covenant community, a body of believers with a mission.

The most straightforward way to comprehend the message is to recall the Biblical drama. God creates the world, chooses a people, delivers them from slavery, makes a covenant with them, gives them a land, and spells out a "law" that is administered by judges, violated by kings, and proclaimed by prophets. The people are exiled, but the dispersed remnant is promised a Messiah, the Servant who inaugurates the new age of the Kingdom of God. The Kingdom is established through the public ministry of the man Jesus, whose love for people and disruption of established order leads to his death as a convict and his victory over the powers of the age as risen Lord. The Kingdom community is moved by a Spirit that works to liberate people and to transform the principalities and powers— in order to establish right human relations. (Notice how "political" are the key Biblical images.)

This knowledge undergirds the community of believers in their willingness to risk insecurity, to bear suffering, to resist evil. Believers know that the powers of sin and evil, which continue to produce collective horrors, social ugliness, and personal misery, shall perish. Though they die hard, these powers are overcome, transcended, defeated. The worst that can happen has happened in the crucifixion and the best is signaled in the resurrection. But this is a painful process, not an automatic occurrence. Jesus was nailed to a cross and hung up to die. True hearers of this story will not romanticize how it happened, or what they must do as disciples. Disciples, of course, are tempted to deny their Lord, but they no longer need be preoccupied with hanging on to their prerogatives and possessions in a frantic effort to avoid insecurity. They have a sense of direction that is determined by God's action in history.

Two Biblical terms especially convey the direction and destination of the divine activity in history. The two terms are: peace and reconciliation. God has reconciled all people as well as all social forces to himself. He is working peace among men. He does it through mighty acts of judgment and mercy that humble the privileged and exalt the deprived. For those who reckon with this movement, the promised outcome is shalom (peace), a term projecting communal wholeness, harmony, integrity—the responsive state of men who are reconciled with God, with nature, with their neighbors, and thus are right with themselves. The church is called to be a community that gathers to celebrate the power of love and the hope of human unity and scatters to demonstrate this common destiny amid social change and conflict.

The Biblical drama remembered here has not lost power, though it is sometimes more appreciated by those outside rather than inside the church. From one generation to the next, people are drawn into the covenant that animates the story. In fact, people who accept this covenant relation find in it their ground of value, their reality picture, their basic context for envisioning the future and responding freely to issues in the present. Their frame of reference is shaped by the costly action of One who breaks through seemingly closed situations to liberate human beings and structures. His promise for the future is signaled especially in the exodus from Egypt and by the death and resurrection of Jesus the Christ.

The Biblical scenario in its covenant context arouses a powerful expectancy of social transformation with a definite preference for political humanism. Today Biblical and political humanism share a similar, though not identical, consciousness of liberation and community which includes the following concepts: [45]

1. To reject the present state of things; to protest poverty, domination, impotence—all forms of oppression;

2. To seek human well-being on the broadest possible basis through creative use of resources;

3. To side with claims of those who are most deprived or disinherited in the nation and worldwide;

4. To show love for both the oppressor and the oppressed, even while opposing unjust powers;

5. To promote social justice through structures of self-development, which emerge from cultural, ethnic, and ideological pluralism;

6. To celebrate the gift of human life together, in the face of a crisis-laden future;

7. To proceed in a manner that recognizes the provisional and ambiguous character of every political act.

How are these goals to be achieved? There is no *one* Christian strategy, warns a report from the Nairobi meeting (August, 1970) of the Reformed Churches:

—There are situations in which we are called to prophetic signposts, pointing unflinchingly to the judgment and truth of Almighty God, regardless of whether or not the world heeds our call. Yet this stance must be taken in deep humility, recognizing that we are always a part of the evil we condemn.

—At other times we must seek relative justice through political persuasion and the agony of compromise. But we must never lose sight of the radical demands of God's kingdom, which can never be subordinated to the powers and principalities of this world.

—The compassion of Jesus Christ may also lead us to a ministry of healing and comforting the afflicted, but this can be no substitute for attacking the root causes of the world's sufferings.

The church at every level can participate in actions which embody its commitment to justice and reconciliation, whether these actions are initiated by Christians or not.

In, through, and beyond the church, in continually surprising places and ways, defatalized groups of people get the spirit. They are determined to help create a human future, with a vision, compassion, and anger informed by the man for others, the man of the new age, Jesus of Nazareth.

This is not to overlook the fact that large segments of the church are demoralized or disoriented. It is to suggest that other segments of the church are quite confident and coherent in their social response. There one can participate in worship and music that speaks to the issues of the new age; creative community services and action programs; legislative advocacy efforts; mini-programs of housing, education, and economic development; as well as theological and political inquiry.

Consider also the church's specialized ministries of dialogue in centers of urban action, business and industry, and higher education. Through them the church can learn

how to relate to other systems and to help powerful institutions meet urgent public needs. The urban action
centers hooked together in the Action Training Coalition
have stimulated church involvement in mass-based community organization and collaboration in programs of
community economic development. The industrial ministries seek to illumine the ethics of corporate decision-
making and to help urban people cross institutional barriers for issue-focused action. They have also facilitated a
process of mediation between low-power groups and the
business establishment. A parallel mode of ministry occurs in the higher educational sector as groups of faculty,
students, and specially trained clergy help universities to
apply their resources in response to the needs of sur-
rounding urban and rural communities. All these approaches to ministry beyond the parish provide keys to
the doors of various societal units. The action efforts that
occur, when publicized, tend to acquire "model power" in
both church and society.

A pluriform church, it turns out, provides one of the
few broad-based, relatively independent networks for communication about, and participation in, the social action
process. This claim should not be exaggerated. Obviously,
much community action effort is spawned by activist
groups of the left and right, by muckraking journalists, by
politically conscious study teams, and by many experienced
public affairs organizations. Some of these action stimu-
lators also have extensive contacts, but they usually lack
widespread support or are in search of new coalitions.
Segments of the church with a nose for homework, a
spirit of freedom, and a willingness to organize can facilitate and multiply social action efforts at local, state, and
national levels. Churches even make an international dif-

ference by reaching across lines of warfare or by seeking to influence policies of government or business overseas.

Without necessarily supplying or underwriting much of the manpower, and without imposing her theological rationale, the church serves in many places and sectors as a midwife for the future. "New life constantly works its way out of old societal forms. The midwife doesn't create the new life, but she serves to facilitate the painful process of birth and to keep an eye on danger signals." [46] This analogy suggests three implications. (1) The midwife chooses which births to assist. (2) A tired or clumsy midwife is of little help. (3) The results of midwifery are uncertain. We see new life and the conditions of birth, but we do not know how the course of events will alter each initiative.

So the church can and should act freely in the present moment. The task is to anticipate outcomes consistent with humane values and to act strategically as befits particular situations, rather than to withdraw to nurse recurrent doubts about being able to do anything at all.

STYLES OF SOCIAL INVOLVEMENT FOUND IN LOCAL CHURCHES

Congregations that report considerable activity in response to social issues vary both in what they do and how they do it. Their behavior reveals that social involvement is a complex (multi-track) process. The following Index of Social Involvement Styles is empirically derived from a study of highly involved United Presbyterian congregations. (The complete report appeared as an Occasional Paper of the United Presbyterian Department of Church and Society. See Dieter Hessel and Les Galbraith, *Socially Involved Congregations,* Occasional Papers on the Church and Conflict, No. 6; Board of Christian Education, The United Presbyterian Church U.S.A., 1971.) Questionnaire data on these congregations was supplemented by in-depth interviews conducted with a pastor and a lay leader in each congregation during 1970. From the results of the interviews, we obtained a clear profile of the social involvement style(s) of forty congregations. The results are presented in the form of an Index on the next two pages.

The Index of Social Involvement Styles (ISIS), viewed horizontally, shows each style to be a configuration of factors A to F. Three factors or components give a profile

INDEX OF SOCIAL INVOLVEMENT STYLES (I

Style	A. *Objective*	B. *Main Activities*	C. *Rationale*
1. Social Service and Dialogue	Aid the casualties; examine attitudes	casework; helping projects	personalistic and pietistic
2. Vicarious Clergy Involvement	Community betterment; personal witness	pastor(s) on civic boards and "at large"	community-relations role
3. Support of Projects	Support service agencies and action organizations	survey needs; grant funds; recruit volunteers	church as corporate citizen
4. Community Center	Comprehensive community development	start and spin-off projects; community facilities	church for all the people
5. Community Action	Self-determination; community organization	dramatize; probe; develop voice in public affairs	church with movement for empowerment
6. Issue-probing; Policy-influencing	Social reform; policy advocacy	organize for timely analysis, influence, and projects	nonpartisan political responsibility
7. Corporate Initiation and Support	Change the system; correct conditions; create options	same as 6, with more planning and corporate support	social transformation as mission priority

D. *Method of Organization*	E. *Available Resources*	F. *Institutional Relationships*
informal or volunteer groups	limited by necessity or habit	approach agencies for individuals
clergy act for the congregation	tied up in church maintenance	through pastor's organizational contacts
committee process for approving project support	offerings; endowments; active laymen	ecumenical or secular agencies initiate plans
major business of congregation's governing board	facilities, location, and leadership, less money	approach government and church agencies for community
cadres work on action for specific gains	seek and receive financing from established agencies	begin with interchurch or movement imperative
task groups design mechanisms and lead action	lay expertise and leadership, but modest funds	monitor agencies; attend hearings; influence deciders
same as 6, with more planning and education	careful deployment of personnel and money	participant in community planning and goal-setting

of *what* the style is, and three indicate *how* it works. Each factor can also be viewed vertically as a continuum with gradations numbering 1 to 7. For example, the objective of local church social involvement can vary all the way from (1) "aid the casualties" to (7) "change the system."

Probably none of the styles as actually practiced "lines up" exactly at the same point on the continuum of all six factors (A to F). But the indicators mentioned in the ISIS were discerned empirically from interviews, and the horizontal readings for each style do fit some real-life congregations.

The order in which the styles are listed in the ISIS reflects three general considerations: (*a*) the increased complexity of higher number styles, (*b*) the larger orbit of higher number styles (extending beyond the immediate church vicinity to settings of metropolitan, state, and national decision), and (*c*) the shift of primary focus from individual *service* to *structural change* efforts, with higher number styles.

The six factors in the ISIS are not the only ones to consider in analyzing social-involvement styles of local churches. For instance, adept pastoral and lay leadership makes a crucial difference. But this is not a separate factor in the Index, since leadership cuts across the *what* and *how* variables and proceeds situationally—in light of the recent history of a congregation and community.

Socioeconomic factors also come into play as a set of *where* variables. These include sex-race-age-class composition, family income, education, political leaning, community setting. Initially, some of these "where" factors were added to the ISIS, but the "where" did not relate in any clear pattern to the "what" and "how" of social-involvement style. It is doubtful that any of these styles characterize churches in only one kind of setting, such as the proverbial "transitional" neighborhood. Although demographic transitions can stimulate or reduce local church action, the complicating fact is that many different demographic transitions are under way throughout contemporary metropolises and in satellite towns.

Variations of a given social-involvement style can occur wherever there is a local church. (This appears to hold true whatever the location or racial composition of a congregation, though we know that well-integrated or predominantly nonwhite congregations are generally more socially activated.) Consequently, "where" factors are excluded from the Index, though some "where" distinctions may be useful in describing a given congregation's style of social involvement.

The ISIS is presented here as a qualitative evaluation and planning aid. When using this Index to analyze a congregation's deeds or intentions, keep in mind the following guidelines:

First, a congregation's social action efforts can encompass more than one style of social involvement simultaneously, though it usually emphasizes one style. Of the forty whose styles could be discerned clearly from the interviews, over half were involved with more than one style or approach. Yet most of them had a clear preference for one style. The forty congregations showed the following stylistic emphases (with congregations showing more than one style classified according to the highest number): style 1—2 congregations; style 2—4 congregations; style 3—12 congregations; style 4—6 congregations; style 5—6 congregations; style 6—7 congregations; style 7—3 congregations.

Second, a congregation's style of social involvement is likely to shift as its leaders learn from previous action efforts. With changes in pastoral and/or lay leadership, the shifts of style can be quite rapid. Several of the congregations interviewed had, under new leadership, only recently begun to respond to social issues with more than a voluntaristic, service-project orientation. The other side of the coin, however, is the tentativeness of much social action. This was reflected in the almost identical comments of laymen in several different situations: "If the pastor left now, our social action efforts would probably fall apart."

Third, the more complex styles depend on technical assistance and financial support from regional and national church agencies as well as from secular agencies. Serious adult education among the membership is also a crucial component of the more complex styles. Keep in mind that social witness and education can occur in connection with all the styles. All the styles can also include nonmembers in their design and implementation.

Fourth, congregations venturing into the more complex styles often continue some of the activities and procedures of the simpler styles. Thus higher number styles tend to encompass some of the lower number styles. Some of the more frequent combinations seem to be: 3 with 1, 4 with 3, 5 with 2, 6 with 3. The lead number indicates the style emphasized. Whether such combinations would also be frequent in less active congregations is a question for further study. Also, we do not know how many congregations have consciously pulled back from more complex to simpler styles.

Some Examples of the Styles

Style 1. A small congregation with predominantly Hispanic membership is now concentrating on nurturing its members and serving individuals who are known to the congregation, in order to help fill the gap in city services and to help persons caught in the culture of poverty. Leaders of the congregation also feel they lack the resources to do much more.

Another congregation with fewer than 150 members, located in a deteriorating neighborhood, is quite active in an interchurch diaconate that focuses on community-wide problems of a smaller city. The combined diaconate develops both service projects (casework and counseling) and community dialogue and action (e.g., regarding such things as the Housing Commission, health services, school integration, tax reforms). A church that could do little by itself is combining elements of style 5 with a vigorous pursuit of style 1 in collaboration with like-minded churches.

Style 2. A public-housing ministry, recently organized into a tiny congregation, is intended to be community-action oriented. But quite a few of the members live in single-parent families and must concentrate on daily survival. The members proudly view the pastor as their main action arm in the community.

A modest center-city congregation with dispersed older membership, still predominantly white, has been startled by several direct action steps of its young pastor (regarding the Indochina war and racial justice). The session has rallied behind the pastor's actions after much soul-searching. Some of the members have transferred their letters, while some younger, change-minded adults have joined.

Style 3. A large congregation with prosperous members in a politically conservative area has begun to shed its reluctance to engage social questions. This is occurring because of adept leadership and by means of an interchurch program to support ministries in special sectors of the metropolis and to link volunteers with appropriate organizations or agencies.

A declining congregation with heavy endowment has decided, by formal session action, to apply its resources to social and human needs throughout the city. Planning for this effort combines a process of adult education with regular review of project proposals and granting of funds (characteristic of style 7). Some members "follow" the money into the organizations being supported.

Style 4. An integrated congregation with consistent pastoral leadership is strategically located to function as a community center. Several agency programs and many community groups (some overtly militant) use the premises. The session is deliberately balanced in socioeconomic composition, holds frequent open meetings with the congregation, and receives strong support. Plans are under way to develop the facilities with housing or a medical clinic. Style 4 blends into style 5 as the session has endorsed community action on questions of welfare, police-community relations, public school policy, and issues of conscience and war.

Style 5. An ecumenically-minded church has launched several community-action projects in housing construction and rehabilitation, educational enrichment, organizing the elderly, a legal-service fund, and an anonymous call-in line for citizens to report crimes without fear of harassment. Financial and personal support for these efforts has come from other churches and secular agencies that became aware of them.

Style 6. A small-town congregation with fewer than three hundred members and with careful pastoral leadership has evolved an adult education program with very high member involvement both locally and in synod. Many social issues are probed in the process and individual volunteers are linked up with service opportunities (style

1). But corporate social witness is also practiced wherever groups of members discover needs too big for them to handle. They have organized letter-writing campaigns and congressional visits on several national issues, devised proposals that were funded in areas such as economic development, low-cost housing, and draft counseling; and have assisted secular groups on other issues. Needless to say, the congregation manifests an air of excitement and confidence.

Style 7. The church and society style develops most fully in a congregation that chooses this mission priority and makes it happen by planning for specific educational and action goals. One congregation moved in this direction with clear goal determination after undergoing a split that exposed its previous incoherence of purpose. This congregation intends to participate directly in community and regional politics and to relate to decision-making structures with hopes of changing the social system where they are.

NOTES

1. Amitai Etzioni, *The Active Society: A Theory of Societal and Political Processes* (The Free Press, 1968), p. 5.

2. Frederick G. Dutton, *Changing Sources of Power: American Politics in the 1970's* (McGraw-Hill Book Co., Inc., 1971), Chs. 2 to 4.

3. Abraham H. Maslow, *Motivation and Personality*, 2d ed. (Harper & Row, Publishers, Inc., 1970). Also see Sidney M. Jourard, *Personal Adjustment* (The Macmillan Company, 1958), for a discussion of the traits of self-actualizing persons: conscious of, and forthright about, reality; accepting of human nature; spontaneous, full of brotherly feeling; relatively autonomous, desirous of periodic privacy; closely related to a few persons; problem-centered, creative; appreciative of the new, unhostile sense of humor; democratic character structure; a strong ethical sense, resistant to conformity.

4. Ralph Nader and Donald Ross, *Action for a Change: A Student's Manual for Public Interest Organizing* (Grossman Publishers, 1971), Pt. One.

5. Rubem Alves, "Some Thoughts on a Program for Ethics," *Union Seminary Quarterly Review,* Vol. 26, No. 2 (Winter, 1971), p. 159.

6. John Platt, "What We Must Do," *Science,* Nov. 28, 1969.

7. William L. Taylor, *Hanging Together: Equality in an Urban Nation* (Simon & Schuster, Inc., Publishers, 1971), p. 192.

8. Christopher Lasch, *The Agony of the American Left* (Alfred A. Knopf, Inc., 1969), pp. 29–30.

9. Etzioni, *op. cit.,* p. 655.

10. Barry Commoner, *The Closing Circle* (Alfred A. Knopf, Inc., 1971), pp. 193, 198.

11. Dieter T. Hessel, *Reconciliation and Conflict: Church Controversy Over Social Involvement* (The Westminster Press, 1969), pp. 23, 36–37, 82.

12. George Crowell, *Society Against Itself* (The Westminster Press, 1968), p. 53.

13. *Ibid.,* pp. 57–58.

14. W. H. Ferry, "The Unanswerable Question," *The Center Magazine,* Vol. II, No. 4 (July, 1969).

15. Saul D. Alinsky, *Rules for Radicals: A Practical Primer for Realistic Radicals* (Random House, Inc., 1971), pp. xviii, xx.

16. My discussion of the "realistic radical" is not drawn from any source, though related insights are to be found in Alinsky, *op. cit.,* and in the following: Arnold S. Kaufman, *The Radical Liberal* (Atherton Press, 1968), Chs. 3 to 4; Peter Berger and Richard Neuhaus, *Movement and Revolution* (Doubleday & Company, Inc., 1970), pp. 142 ff.; and Michael Novak, *The Experience of Nothingness* (Harper & Row, Publishers, Inc., 1970), Ch. 4, The "older" realism to which I refer has its most classic formulation in the writings of Reinhold Niebuhr. A modified and somewhat radicalized version of Christian realism developed in the thought of John Bennett and is summarized by Robert Lee in *The Promise of Bennett: Christian Realism and Social Responsibility* (J. B. Lippincott Company, 1969), Ch. III.

17. Benjamin DeMott, *Surviving the 70's* (E. P. Dutton & Co., Inc., 1971), pp. 11–12.

18. Herbert Blumer, "Social Problems as Collective Behavior," *Social Problems,* Vol. 18, No. 3 (Winter, 1971), argues that social problems have their being not so much in objective conditions as in an unstudied process of collective definition.

19. Robert Bonthius, "So—You Want to Change the System?" *Trends,* Oct., 1971, p. 28. Bonthius identifies four action steps: (1) Analysis: What is our social problem? (2) Goal setting: What is our action goal? (3) Strategy: What is

our plan of action? and (4) Evaluation: What are the results? What do we do next?

20. John P. Spiegel, "Theories of Violence: An Integrated Approach," *International Journal of Group Tensions,* Vol. 1, No. 1 (Jan.–March, 1971), p. 77.

21. See Kenneth D. Benne and Max Birnbaum, "Principles of Changing," in Warren G. Bennis, Kenneth D. Benne, and Robert Chin (eds.), *The Planning of Change,* 2d ed. (Holt, Rinehart and Winston, Inc., 1969).

22. Alinsky, *op. cit.,* pp. 58, 119–120.

23. Bonthius, *loc. cit.,* p. 30.

24. Henry Clark, *Ministries of Dialogue: The Church Confronts the Power Structures* (Association Press, 1971), Appendix, "Conceptual Tools for Effective Strategy Planning," p. 206.

25. Robert Theobald, *An Alternative Future for America II* (The Swallow Press, Inc., 1970), pp. 23–24.

26. George D. Younger, "Direct Action and Public Policy," a paper for the Krisheim Institute on Social Involvement (Board of Christian Education, The United Presbyterian Church U.S.A., 1968), mimeographed.

27. Charles V. Hamilton, "How Black Is Black?" *Ebony,* Aug. 1969, pp. 48 f.

28. Max L. Stackhouse, "Whatever Happened to Reparations?" *Andover Newton Quarterly,* Nov. 1970.

29. Clark, *op. cit.,* Ch. 4.

30. Alinsky, *op. cit.,* pp. 126–127.

31. Gabriel J. Fackre, *Liberation in Middle America* (Pilgrim Press, 1971), Ch. 8.

32. Alinsky, *op. cit.,* pp. 24 ff.

33. Rudolf Heberle, *Social Movements: Introduction to Political Sociology* (Appleton-Century-Crofts, Inc., 1951), Ch. 16.

34. Robert McAfee Brown, "Nonviolence in a Violent World," *Presbyterian Life,* June 1, 1971, p. 26. Also see Charles West, *Ethics, Violence and Revolution* (Council on Religion and International Affairs, Special Studies #208, 1969), and my discussion of the realistic radical, Chapter 4, above.

35. Hannah Arendt, "Reflections on Civil Disobedience," *The New Yorker,* Sept. 12, 1970.

36. Edward LeRoy Long, Jr., *Confrontation in Harrisburg: Some Guidelines for Reflection,* Occasional Papers on the Church and Conflict, No. 7 (Board of Christian Education, The United Presbyterian Church U.S.A.), pp. 42–43. Also see Mulford Q. Silbey, *The Obligation to Disobey: Conscience and the Law* (CRIA, Special Studies #209, 1970).

37. Etzioni, *op. cit.,* pp. 286–288, calls this decision-making strategy a "mixed-scanning" approach, such as the infantry scanning a field or a good chess player pondering the board.

38. E.g., "Report Says 10 Churches Abet 'Immoral Acts' of Arms Industry," *The New York Times,* Jan. 5, 1972. This news story refers to a report of the Corporate Information Center, *Church Investments, Technological Warfare, and the Military-Industrial Complex* (National Council of Churches, 1972).

39. See Charles Powers, *Social Responsibility and Investments* (Abingdon Press, 1971), and "The Church and American Corporations," *Church and Society,* March–April, 1972.

40. Haskell M. Miller, *Social Welfare Ministries in a Time of Radical Social Change—A Report to the Churches for the 1970's* (National Council of Churches, 1970). Criteria for self-development grants by the United Presbyterian Church appear in *Church and Society,* Jan.–Feb., 1971, pp. 55 ff.

41. Douglass W. Johnson and Nordon C. Murphy, *Punctured Preconceptions: What North American Christians Think of Their Church* (Friendship Press, 1972).

42. Jeffrey K. Hadden, *The Gathering Storm in the Churches* (Doubleday & Company, Inc., 1969), p. 17. Also see Joseph C. Hough, Jr., "The Church Alive and Changing," *The Christian Century,* Jan. 5, 1972.

43. *Social Action,* Jan., 1972, pp. 12–15.

44. As indicated in unpublished research by Dean R. Hoge, of Princeton Seminary.

45. Rubem Alves, *A Theology of Human Hope* (Corpus Books, 1969), focuses on the reciprocal relationship between Biblical and political humanism.

46. Gaylord B. Noyce, *The Responsible Suburban Church* (The Westminster Press, 1970), p. 155.